THE BRAND AVATAR

Unlock Your Professional Potential
& Dramatically Increase Your Income

Duane Browne & Raymond Aaron

AuthoritiesPress

Publisher
10-10-10 Publishing
Markham, ON
Canada

Printed in Canada and the United States of America

Table of Contents

Dedication

First and always foremost, thank you **Lord Jesus** for blessing me, and I pray you continue to use me to bless others with humility.

To my amazing daughter, **Imani**, who teaches me the importance of the creative mind, laughter, and unconditional love, every day. You are going to impact the world in a positive way and your mother and I will stop at nothing to give you all the tools to accomplish it.

To my Godchildren, **Remi** and **Ezra**, I hope you see all the possibilities that life has to offer. I pray that you strive to attain all your goals and dreams. May you have the success that you want throughout your lives and give thanks at every opportunity.

Foreword

Where branding has been the focus of companies for decades, Duane Browne takes branding to the individual level in *The Brand Avatar: Unlock Your Professional Potential & Dramatically Increase Your Income*. This guide gives young professionals the skills and wisdom to take their careers to the next level.

Right from the start, Duane helps you to focus on your goals, allowing you to create a plan for where you want to go and how to get there. He guides you through the process of creating your own brand avatar, including stories and examples that effectively illustrate the points.

Throughout *The Brand Avatar*, Duane gives you tips on when to stand out and when to step back. His experience shines through in his tools for addressing how you are perceived by those you work with and those who can provide opportunities for you to advance your career. If you are looking for the ultimate guide to stand out and dramatically increase your income while advancing your career, then *The Brand Avatar* is the book for you!

Loral Langemeier
The Millionaire Maker

Introduction

What is a Brand Avatar and What Makes a Great Brand?

*"What does your attitude proclaim
to the world about you today?
It is never too late to change your story, start by changing
your thoughts, and pay attention to your attitude."*
– Bob Proctor

Standing out in a professional setting is key to helping people remember who you are, and to increasing your level of influence. In the professional realm of your office, there are multiple settings where you have the opportunity to make a mark. The question is, what kind of mark are you leaving? Are you that individual everyone wants on their team because of the qualities and skills that you bring, or are you the one that everyone hopes is assigned somewhere else?

Just a heads up, if you don't know anyone who everyone tends to avoid working with, you are probably that person. It is possible to change that, but like anything else, it is going to involve making an effort to change your presentation, and thereby alter the perception that people have of you.

Think about your favorite online game or social media site. In those virtual worlds, where you can decide who you are, what you look like, and how you want to present yourself, your avatar becomes an extension of who you are and what you want to achieve. Now I want you to apply those same principles to your career. Building a brand avatar is about making conscious choices regarding how you want to present yourself, and the perception that you want to create. Online, you might be able to fake it, but in real life, you can't fake it. Building a brand avatar is about being what they want online and offline, even if your true offline self does not exactly *align* with what they want.

When it comes to your career and professional advancement, you cannot ignore how they impact each other. Simply put, there is no divide between the aspects of your personal and professional lives. One will always reflect on the other. With that in mind, it is important to address who you are online and offline, and brand yourself, not only as you want to be perceived, but also based on what you want to achieve.

Whether you know it or not, everything is branding. From the clothes you wear, how you react to situations, and even what you eat, everything is a statement about your brand. In other books, I have said the same thing about marketing, but after working in marketing and branding for over 15 years in numerous industries, I can say the statement is correct for marketing and branding alike.

Marketing is to branding what an artist is to art. Marketing is all the combined efforts to solidify, maintain, or enhance your brand. Branding is the by-product of all those efforts. Many people think branding is limited to products or services, but remember, everything is branding. If everything is branding, then the way you market yourself for success is no exception. The way prospects, colleagues, clients, and competitors perceive you is a direct function of branding.

Misty was talented, and she had plenty of good ideas that would have created many opportunities for her company to expand their business. But Misty was also not a talker. In fact, most people thought she was standoffish, and so she wasn't making the connections that she needed to advance in the company. Her company was full of loud and direct individuals who shared their ideas, and meetings included multiple points of view before decisions were made. Except one voice was rarely heard. You guessed it: Misty's!

Now, do you think that her career was heading up like she planned? No, it wasn't, simply because she was falling below the radar. Her company's culture didn't match up to parts of her personality and, instead of adapting, Misty was falling behind, and not feeling empowered to take the reins in her career.

Then Misty decided to make some changes. She was ready to take her career to a new place, but she realized that if she didn't start sharing her ideas, that was never going to happen. It meant a change in mindset for Misty. Creating her brand avatar was about changing the perception that she didn't have ideas, by being more vocal during meetings. She took the time to share and, once she did, her ideas started to get acknowledged. Her voice grew in the company, and it translated into a promotion. It wasn't that Misty gained new skills or suddenly got better at her job. She just met the company culture where it was, and the result was that she contributed to her own success.

The problem with many people who fall short of their professional or personal goals is they overlook how others perceive them. Sometimes people view themselves in a light that the world does not see. Right or wrong, positive or negative, perception is reality; and how the outside world views you is your brand to them. Even as I entered the marketing industry, I at times also missed the importance and power of personal branding.

When I was in university, I had a chip on my shoulder, being one of the only people of color in the class. I would not network much with others, and usually stayed by myself and studied alone. For me, I thought everyone felt I was not worthy to be there. The reality was my personal brand was perceived as closed off, unfriendly, and a loner. It wasn't until I had to work in groups that other students saw the real me. I was someone who enjoyed taking a lead in presentations, and I loved the marketing process.

During my career, I have missed out on countless opportunities because I had either discounted, dismissed, or plum forgot that 100% of my conduct, couture, and concepts should be branded consciously. I can remember when I was a marketing manager for a multimillion-dollar company that did not have a dress code. I loved it because I could come to work in jeans, and the company was focused on my output and not so much on my appearance. The mistake in that thinking was illustrated by the fact that even though the VP allowed for casual dress code, he wore suits every day. When he walked in the room, people noticed he was present, because he stood out. He dressed for success (and was a success), so the question was, what was I dressing for?

Truth be told, when I am home alone, there is nothing more comfortable than wearing a pair of jogging pants and a V-neck shirt. Now, I do own suits, but my comfort clothing is sports gear. On top of that, I love my hip-hop music. When I am driving home from almost any place in my car, you better believe I have old school hip hop playing (semi-loud I may add), with me nodding my head to the tunes coming out of the stereo. At the time, I worked at one of Canada's top telecommunication companies, and if they had known the full extent of the true me, I am pretty sure they would not have hired me. To some degree, I was already a brand avatar.

For some, the idea of re-inventing themselves, or not being faithful to their *true* selves, seems almost impossible given their life's reality. Well, the great news I bring to you today is this book should help provide you with the guidance and resources to become successful in any industry and, at the same time, allow you to be true to yourself. This is possible through the concept of creating your own avatar to be the vessel to your personal branding requirements. This book is for anyone who is looking for a change in the way they view themselves, or the way people view them.

Are you one of those people who can't seem to understand why you never get that promotion when you are the most qualified?

Or maybe you are one of those people who feels like you never seem to fit into the cookie cutter mold that society or your profession has for you?

Lastly, you may be that person who has no interest in *"selling out"*, or not being yourself in the world. I find many individuals I have coached usually fall into one of those categories. Then there is another segment of people I coach, who have always played by the rules, who get promotions but look to supercharge their career and stand out within their respective industry. Whichever segment you best identify with, the ability to craft that perfect perception to display to the world will be your greatest asset in your quest for success in everything you do. Owning your brand avatar will accomplish just that for anyone willing to follow the instructions embedded on these pages.

What is an avatar? More importantly, what is a brand avatar? If you have not had the chance to watch the blockbuster movie, *Avatar*, by James Cameron, I urge you to do so to gain some more context on the topic of an Avatar. The premise of the movie was the ability of a soldier to transport his mind into the body of a genetically engineered host body, in order to blend in and interact with the natives of a foreign land.

A more detailed version is a soldier who lost the ability of his legs, but he used his ability to think and act like the enemy, as the main weapon to defeat the natives of a foreign land. This was accomplished by transporting the mind of the soldier into a body the army created to resemble the natives. Once his mind was in this vessel, he was able to walk, talk, look, and act like the natives, which allowed the army to gain intelligence on what would be required to defeat them and claim their land. By no means am I suggesting an avatar with negative connotations. Instead, I was highlighting that the ability to utilize an avatar is how someone was able to transform their reality and become a new person—one who matches the perception of what success looks like.

Now, when we expand that logic to branding, you can begin to understand the concept of this book with more clarity. A brand avatar can:

- Allow the shy introvert to command a stage and give an amazing presentation.
- Allow the ex-con to be viewed as the most trusted business partner.
- Transform the disgruntled factory worker into management material.

No matter if it is your professional or personal goals and desires, creating a brand avatar gives you the flexibility to turn on and off the perception you want the world to have of you. The ability to do this in an increasingly judgemental and competitive world is an amazing weapon you can have at your disposal. I am going to share a personal truth to help drive home this fact. Some of you have heard me present on stage, and some of you have read about some of my business ventures. Well, all those activities required me to put on my power suit, shine up my wing toe shoes, and eliminate all facial hair. I do this to personify what success *may* look like. Now, my personal view is that success comes from work, not presentation, but since everyone is judged in the first 10–15 seconds, I have to look like a success. If you are one of my friends (which I hope anyone reading these pages will seek to stay in touch), you already know that shaving and wearing dress clothes are things I fight with on a daily basis. I prefer to wear shorts and T-shirts, but there is a time and place for everything.

Taking things an important step further, you want your overall persona to exceed that of whatever the status quo is. If you are wearing a suit at an event, it does nothing for you if your suit is too baggy, or if you are not aware of dinner party etiquette. When creating your brand avatar, make a game out of it, and have fun with your avatar. All successful actors study their role and get into character to deliver an amazing performance. That is the same way you need to view your brand avatar. It is a role you are playing where you need to act the part. The great thing about becoming your brand avatar is that it is up to you how long you stay in character. This process will allow you to facilitate the desired brand perception in your industry and, at the same time, allow you to step outside that reality if you so wish, to just be yourself.

No matter where you work, your company is conscious about its brand personality, which includes what people are saying about the company and its brands. If you translate that to your brand, then it is clear you need to be aware of what is being said about you online, but also about what connections you are making and what impact your brand presence is having.

Think about that idea of an avatar. You want it to reflect who you are, your values, beliefs, and purpose. Throughout this book, I want you to focus on what you are putting out there that is impacting your brand. Are you crafting the right message for the goals you want to achieve, or is the message falling flat and missing your audience altogether?

As a professional looking to grow in your career and make significant strides, you need to be focused on not only what you are communicating but how you are communicating it. Too often, it is a case of focusing in on a few details but missing the bigger picture of how all those aspects impact your brand. There is an often-toted expression that you cannot see the forest for the trees. I want you to get into the mindset of seeing the forest, not just a few individual trees. Recognize that you cannot have a silo mentality to branding.

I want you to learn from successful companies, see what they do right and what they do wrong, and then use it as a guide. This book is focused on distilling those examples, giving you the knowledge to build a brand for yourself that gives you the platform to achieve your goals. So, what makes a brand successful? There are a few key aspects that you need to consider.

1. Most successful brands know their audience, specifically their target demographic.
2. A brand needs to be unique, not a copycat.
3. You need to have a passion for your brand to sustain it long-term.
4. You need consistency in message.
5. No successful brand is stagnant but is always trying to improve.
6. Brands have multiple avenues to gain access to their target audience.
7. You need a leader that can act on behalf of the brand, and steer it successfully to reach goals and milestones.

Note how each of these aspects can apply to your personal brand. We will be talking about them all in the context of your personal and professional brand, but before we can talk about how to apply these things, you need to know what your brand is. I want you to be able to take these tools and use them to reach the next level in your career and your life!

It is an exciting time to be a professional, as there are multiple avenues available for you to grow your brand, and to grow personally and professionally. I am excited to take this journey with you, so let's get started!

Part 1

The Beginning of Creating a Winning You

Chapter 1

Who is the REAL You?

"Our true self is being who we are."
– Lailah Gifty Akita

What you will learn:

- Getting to know the real you
- Understand what branding means
- What your true perception is in the world, and how it impacts your ability to grow professionally

Before I can even begin to help you brand yourself in a way that will rocket you upward in your career, you need to determine who you are and what you want your brand to be. It is so easy to go through life following a path defined by others, never exploring who you are or where you want to go. The media, social, and cultural expectations can steer you on a course that takes you on a journey that leaves you feeling frustrated and unfulfilled.

It is so easy to follow a path defined by others. After all, the path of least resistance can provide a pleasant journey, but it lacks the excitement which comes from achieving a goal based on your hard work, or the joy that results from overcoming a hurdle or challenge.

Many of you learned to ride a bike when you were younger. It was difficult at first, learning how to balance the bike to keep yourself moving forward perfectly. Success was not immediate. I am sure that you fell several times and might even have felt like giving up. Still, your parents were there to encourage you, guide you, and even run beside you, holding that seat. Eventually, they let go, and you had that moment of pure joy when you realized that you were riding your bike! Of course, learning to stop was something else.

I want you to feel that joy in your professional life, but the only way to do so is to define who you are, what you are capable of, and the direction that you want to go. It might mean stretching yourself mentally and physically, but the results can be amazing.

Do You REALLY Know the Real You?

Think of yourself as a ship. The best captains know their ships inside and out. They know what their ship is capable of and how to get the best out of it in any situation and in any weather condition. Then there are the captains that let their ship be cared for by others. They don't know the ins and outs of their ship, leaving them blind to its abilities when difficult conditions arise. What type of captain are you in your professional life?

I want you to start your journey by taking the time to get to know yourself. Write down what you value, what inspires you, what gets you excited, and what brings you joy. Here are a few questions to get you started:

- What is your purpose in life?
- How does your career compliment that, or do you need to create a professional shift?
- What do you bring to the table for your company? How can you benefit them?

- What do your employers think of you?
- What qualities or skills do you want them to associate with you?

When you start to think about and focus on these aspects of who you are, then you also start to identify the influences that play a part in creating and defining your beliefs and how you operate in the world, as well as what values shape your priorities, including what you focus your energy on. If you find joy in a specific task or experience, then you are going to create the circumstances that allow you to enjoy that experience time and time again.

At the same time, without a clear picture of who you are, it can be easy for external influences to come into play. I have seen individuals steered on a course that ends up leaving them feeling frustrated and unhappy in their professional lives, simply because they did not know what they wanted, and they did not clearly define their goals.

You need to step in and define yourself before others do it for you. Once you know who you are, then you can begin to shape how people perceive you, which is going to become the essence of your brand. Remember, the avatar spent time learning about the people and culture that he was infiltrating. Still, it was his mind, his thoughts, and his values that played a part in the decisions he made. Although he presented himself in a certain way, in the end, he behaved consistently true to who he was.

Be honest and ask yourself:

- Why do I work where I work?
- What factored into my decision?
- Was it the location, money, convenience, or the chance to work with someone in particular?
- What do you like about the environment?

These questions are meant to help you truly understand why you made your choice. Too often, you can decide for a superficial reason, and then find that you hate your job. To be real, you hate your job because you know it is not where you are supposed to be. The question is, why did you do that? Finding the answer gives you the ability to start making real changes.

You may have personal limitations, ones that you may feel are stopping you from moving forward. An avatar mentality allows you to play to your strengths and take on qualities that magnify your abilities. Remember the shy individual who stands up and speaks in front of a large crowd?

I do not want you to automatically assume that if you are not as skilled in one area or another, that it limits your ability to reach your goals or achieve your dreams. It is your moment to accept the challenge and allow yourself to grow, just like you did on that bike so many years ago.

Recognizing both your strengths and weaknesses can help you as you begin the process of branding yourself. If you don't understand who you are, it is impossible to craft a brand. The best brands have a clear definition and message, one that is not confused by the various elements presented. Let's focus on defining branding, and how it can impact you!

Branding – The marketing practice of creating a name, symbol, or design that identifies and differentiates a product, company, or individual from all others.

Branding Defined

When you are creating a brand, the goal is to give yourself an edge in a marketplace that has grown even more competitive. In your professional life, there are dozens of people who want to move up, and they are all displaying a unique set of skills, knowledge, and experience. What is going to make you stand apart in that crowd? It is your brand and the strategy that you use to implement it.

Your brand becomes a promise that you are making to your employer and those that you work with every day. You are telling them what they can expect from you, in terms of values, work ethic, and ability to push yourself to succeed. At the same time, you are telling them what you can offer them that sets you apart from a crowd. It is how you want people to perceive you, who you are, and who you want to be.

In your company, what sets you apart? What makes you stand out? Keep in mind, you cannot please everyone and be all things to all people. Therefore, you have to define the message that you want to send, and then take action to enforce that message.

Stop for a second and think about a scavenger hunt. In order to move forward, you have to figure out the clues, but that also means that the original clues can't be so cryptic that no one can figure them out. Make your message clear, and give clues to who you are, so that you can lead your potential employers to the right conclusions about where you are headed in your career. What makes you stand out should be consistently communicated across all areas of your professional life.

However, having a brand includes more than just having a consistent message. It is having a strategy to deliver that message across a variety of platforms. From your social media to the skills and education you choose to pursue, all of it needs to be part of your brand strategy. Recognize that where you choose to emphasize your brand is just as important as what you emphasize about your brand.

Consistency in strategic branding will give you strong brand equity, adding value to your professional career. It is that value that will help you to jump forward in your career, blasting you toward your goals and what you want to achieve. The value you bring to your company also means that you put yourself in a position to demand more compensation in exchange for what you offer them.

As you start to grow in your career, you are going to add new skills, knowledge, and experience. Doing so will mean that you need to adjust your brand strategy from time to time, but the overall brand message needs to be consistent to your purpose, values, beliefs, and goals.

Once you have defined your brand and what you want to say, then you need to start picking the best methods to bring that message to the forefront. Use your brand avatar as your ambassador, allowing you to implement your brand strategy effectively.

Part of your brand strategy might include expanding your network, both within your industry and outside of it. While it might not seem advantageous to step outside of your industry, doing so can expose you to new opportunities that you might not have considered in the past. Those opportunities could be the ones that help you to propel your career forward!

Additionally, stepping outside your industry can allow you to present your brand avatar to a new audience, creating a fresh perception of you and your abilities, skills, and experience.

It can be so easy to see your skills, knowledge, and experience only from the frame of your current industry. That same set of skills, knowledge, and experience could translate very well to another industry if you are willing to be open-minded to the opportunities out there.

You are going to have multiple options to integrate your brand avatar into your professional world. It starts with all aspects of your life, even down to the message left on your phone's voicemail. All of it has to work in concert with your brand as part of a larger strategy. Your brand avatar needs to showcase the message and present you in the best light for the goals you want to achieve.

- What is your voice?
- Are you going to be known for a friendly tone, or a more business-like and brisker one?
- How are you presenting yourself to others in professional situations?
- Are you communicating a message that is consistent with your goals?

The point is that your communication, regardless of the platform, needs to be consistent. Doing so, you create a brand that people will begin to identify with you, and it will also help them to define their expectations of you in the workplace.

One thing that you need to be aware of is that you can damage your brand as easily as you can improve it, simply by not delivering as promised. In your company, you are known by what you produce, as well as how you work with others to achieve the goals of the company. As you build your brand, it is important to understand how individuals within the organization perceive you, and then work to improve that perception or risk damaging it.

What is the TRUE Perception of You in the World?

Why is it so critical to understand how you are perceived in your professional life? Simply put, because how you are perceived is going to positively or negatively impact your brand avatar and your ability to fast track your career. It is not about what you think they perceive about you, but what they actually do perceive about you.

The problem with perception is that it is very easy to have it altered by another person's experiences and viewpoints, even if they have only limited interactions with you or have only just met you. Your brand, as you consistently communicate it, will begin to shape or even shift the perceptions people have of you as a professional. Do not be quick to assume that a perception cannot be changed.

- Are you out of school and looking for work?
- Were you recently laid off from your current vocation?
- Maybe you are in the process of looking to do a career change, or preparing for a job interview?
- Further still, maybe you're tired of other *under-qualified* people getting the job you feel you deserve?

If any of these scenarios speaks to you, then this book was created for you. All of life's interactions with people boil down to personal branding. If you feel you are not winning in the game of life, it could be the current state of your personal brand. Jay-Z (an entertainment mogul worth millions) said, "I'm not a businessman. I'm a business, man!" What he was trying to convey was that everything he does, from when he wakes up in the morning to the time he goes to sleep at night, is calculated and deliberate. He understands that successful personal branding is what separated him from the masses. The interesting thing about Jay-Z is, he went from a low-life drug dealer on the corner, to a multimillion-dollar businessman, controlling and operating legitimate global operations. Sometimes you can find him wearing a big gold chain, sneakers, and a New York fitted baseball cap. At other times, you will see him wearing a fine tailored suit at an exclusive political event. Different circles view Jay-Z in different ways, and he recognizes that and acts accordingly, depending on the various environments he is in.

Understanding personal branding is not about selling out or being fake or unauthentic. Personal branding is about knowing your environment and knowing how and when to blend in, and how and when to stand out and be a leader.

First impressions are made within seconds of your interactions with people. Once someone has formed an opinion about you, your abilities or inabilities, it can be extremely difficult to change that impression they have formed of you. Warren Buffett said, "It takes 20 years to build a reputation, and five minutes to ruin it. If you think about that, you'll do things differently."

Other people's perceptions of you may be the roadblock preventing you from being successful in life and/or in business. You may be aware of these perceptions, or even more concerning, you may not even be aware of perceptions that people have of you. The good news is you have the power to change those perceptions. Other people's perceptions of you, right or wrong, can be changed by taking action.

Three common negative perceptions of people are:

1. They are lazy.
2. They are unprofessional.
3. They lack intelligence.

If someone thinks you are lazy, they may be correct (contrary to what you think your reality is). Are you doing everything you can and should be doing in your career and personal life? If the perception of laziness is not true, try taking more initiative with tasks, to create cognitive dissonance in those who may feel you are lazy. Ask for more responsibilities than required, and go above and beyond the call of duty. Let your accomplishments shine through your actions. If you have a skill, display it. Let people know you have value. Going a step further, watch your body language. Be alert, confident, and assertive. The way you carry yourself could play into the perception that you are lazy, simply because you appear to slouch, with your head down and a zoned-out look on your face.

Part of creating a change in perception is being consciously aware of how you are presenting yourself. Think about your body language, your facial expressions, and even your tone of voice. All of these things contribute to people's perceptions of you, and when you make changes to these areas, you create a dissonance that makes people stop and look again. Not everyone will change their perception, but enough will that it can impact your professional life in a positive and game-changing way.

According to Merriam-Webster[1], professionalism is defined as "the conduct, aims, or qualities that characterize or mark a profession or a professional person; the following of a profession (such as athletics) for gain or livelihood." Many of us think we know what professionalism is, but the question is, are you implementing that into your brand avatar? If, like me, you enjoy a casual work environment, are you truly the most casual person in the office? Could someone look at you and not be sure that you weren't in your pajamas?

One of the ways to define if you are behaving professionally is to look around your office. How are others that you would deem professional behaving? What habits do they have, and what behavior do they display? Mentors are also helpful in dissecting your behavior and giving you constructive criticism about how well you are displaying professionalism.

Even if you are fairly professional, there are definitely ways to improve, thus benefiting your brand avatar and your career.

- Increase your professionalism:
- Improve your etiquette, in public and private.
- Be courteous; it's contagious.
- Smile and others will reciprocate.
- Be open to criticism, and filter your responses for unwelcome comments.

If you feel you lack professionalism, try to drastically improve your etiquette, both in public and when no one is around watching (even if you already consider yourself a master). When you are polite and

[1] https://www.merriam-webster.com/dictionary/professionalism

respectful, then it is more difficult for people to judge, blame, or disrespect you unfairly. Sometimes professionalism comes from a sense of conscious constraint. What my grandmother used to tell me is true: God gave me two ears, two eyes, and one mouth for a reason, which is to talk less while doubling my listening ability, and watching what is happening around me.

If the perception is that you are unintelligent, then speak up and share your opinions. Let people know you are in the room, and you have quality opinions and can add to conversations and ideas. You can have all the intelligence and credentials in the world, but if you are not willing to share your thoughts, ideas, and vision, then no one will draw it out for you.

I remember when I was just starting in my marketing career, I used to become a mute once our VP walked in the room. He was a very intimidating individual who commanded attention as soon as he walked in the room. In my first interaction with him, I witnessed him make a grown man cry at a meeting, for sharing incorrect data with the team. After that, I was afraid to say the wrong things or share my opinion on matters. In retrospect, two things happened. One, I branded him an intimidating force to be reckoned with (which was not his intended brand after speaking to him years later regarding the matter). Second, my brand was perceived by many as timid, and someone who lacked initiative (which was far from the brand I wanted to convey, as I did have many creative ideas to share with the team).

These, and many more themes, will play out in this book, but what you should take from this is that you are the leader of your destiny, you are the leader of your life! It does not matter if you are an introvert or extrovert, you are the leader of everything you do, and you ultimately control the perception other people have of you. The term, *leader*, a lot of the time, is used to describe bosses, managers, celebrities, and innovators. These people guide, motivate, instruct, and strategize the world we live in. If they guide us, then you are the leader of yourself.

You spend 24 hours a day, 7 days a week, being the leader of your mind, body, and soul. You decide your thoughts, you decide your actions, and you determine the way you would like others to view you. Being a leader is more than just a title; when it comes to your destiny, being a leader is mandatory. If you are the leader of your life, what does that look like? Being the leader of your life can take on many forms and shapes. Given the fact this book intends to help create and/or maintain an amazing personal brand, the idea of leadership can take the form of:

- **Someone who guides**: Leaders help look for areas of weakness in yourself, and actively seek to change it or use it as an advantage.
- **Someone who gives credit**: Leaders have the ability to acknowledge your strengths and celebrate your successes, no matter how small the accomplishments may seem.
- **Someone who provides vision:** Leaders help to provide a complete path to success.
- **Someone who enlightens**: Leaders help show the importance of education and development required to get you to the end goal.
- **Someone who inspires**: Leaders motivate, which leads to action and inspiration, through positive reinforcement.
- **Someone who is the authority**: Leaders are great at coming up with answers to problems, or guiding others to paths to solve problems (directly or indirectly).

You have the ability and power to take how people view you professionally or personally and transform it into whatever you like. You are the leader and master of your tomorrow. It may sound a bit idealistic or impossible, but with conscious effort and following instructions required to succeed, you can change how people view you, and rebrand yourself. Being the leader of your life, you can direct your life to manifest such results, simply by creating a *brand avatar* for yourself.

If You Had a Magic Wand, Who Would You Be?

At this moment, you have the pieces of the puzzle that you need to determine the type of brand you want to have. But your brand does not have to be limited to a few short-term career moves. It can encompass every part of your life.

Right now, I want you to wave a magic wand and tell me who you would be if there were no barriers, and nothing stood in your way. What would you do? Where would you live? How would you impact others? All of these aspects are part of who you are and will flow naturally outward into your brand. Do not try to hide who you are, but instead, focus on how you can have a positive impact on your world by letting your true self shine.

Wrap Up for Chapter 1 (Who is the REAL You?)

- Branding starts by understanding who you are and what you want to achieve, then creating a plan to communicate that message consistently and effectively to your target audience.
- You need to have a vision of your future to create a branding plan.
- Perception is key, and you can influence how others perceive you.
- Do not limit your brand to your professional life. Allow it to be part of every aspect of your life.

Understanding yourself is just the first step, but more is involved. There needs to be a conscious effort to act in harmony with that vision of yourself. Thoughts need to lead to actions that can create change. To do that, you need to be willing to make changes to your mindset, giving yourself a foundation to take your brand avatar to the next level in achieving your dreams. With that as our focus, let's *get set to adjust your mindset!* In this next chapter, I will focus on what a conscious branding mindset is and how you can create it, the importance of consistency in all areas of your brand, and how to define your vision and voice to create that consistency, in order to help you excel with your brand avatar.

Chapter 2

Get Set to Adjust Your Mindset

**"Once your mindset changes,
everything on the outside will change along with it."
– Steve Maraboli, author of *Life, the Truth, and Being Free***

What you will learn:

- What a conscious branding mindset is, and how you create it
- The importance of consistency in all areas of your brand
- Defining your vision and voice to create consistency in your brand message

Your mindset is critical to how you approach everything in your career, especially your brand avatar. If you do not have the right mindset, it will be difficult to impossible for you to make the career jumps and boosts that will take you where you want to go. However, the right mindset can help you to achieve more than you might have even thought was possible.

With that in mind, you need to look at the choices you are making, and whether they are positively or negatively impacting your vision of your career and where you want to go. Let's start with focusing on how you create a conscious branding mindset.

Create a Conscious Branding Mindset

Changing your mindset to function as your brand avatar is more than just walking the walk and talking the talk. Developing a successful brand avatar first requires you to have a branding mindset. As part of that, you need to develop and strengthen your intuition to know when you should be aware of your surroundings, and the perception you want to convey in that environment or situation.

Every situation or environment that you find yourself in requires you to determine the perception you want to create of yourself.

"Social media is changing the way we communicate
and the way we are perceived, both positively and negatively.
Every time you post a photo or update your status, you are
contributing to your own digital footprint and personal brand."
– Amy Jo Martin

Think about a party for instance. Perhaps you are going out with several close friends to celebrate a birthday. The perception of being fun-loving, outgoing, and even goofy might be just right for that situation of celebration. Now imagine that you are going to another party, one where you are celebrating the promotion of a colleague. While you still are going to be celebrating, you might not want to be perceived as goofy during this particular event.

The point is that you must honest with yourself about the type of perception you want to leave with individuals, and that can be largely determined by the environment, who is present, and how that perception can impact your brand avatar.

I don't want you to be stiff and not enjoy yourself, because that defeats the purpose of creating the best perception of yourself. When you enjoy what you do, it shows, and others can see it in how you carry yourself, and in the passion that shines through your voice, facial expressions, and actions. Still, there is a time and a place for everything. Part of your brand avatar's role is to understand that concept and then allow you to act accordingly.

Now let's talk about taking what you do seriously. You might enjoy what you do, but if you aren't perceived as taking your work seriously, then it can backfire on you. Far too often, individuals get sidetracked, losing their motivation and not keeping up the hard work. Do not allow yourself to stop thinking that you can skate on your previous accomplishments. You need to always focus on how you can improve what you did in the past.

Think of the term, *failing forward*. What does that really mean? It means taking failure and using it as a learning opportunity, and then making substantial changes to address the issues resulting from that failure. Doing so can lead to success—a true shift in how you are perceived by others.

You then must have an honest conversation with your true self to see where your comfort level is with this perception. Creating this conscious branding mindset takes time, dedication, and persistence to strengthen your brand avatar. The good news is, there are a host of various ways to help speed up your successful results. Below are various methods, which require little effort on your part but ask you to focus on blending in with your environment. It is best to first try one of the methods below that best match your personality.

Here are the three areas I am going to focus on, which I call the 3 A's:

- Appearance
- Association
- Achievement

Let's start with appearance. You are going to an amazing restaurant, one that has a menu to die for, with a chef that receives rave reviews.

Placing your order takes time because there are so many amazing options. Once you make your decision, you wait for that meal, your mouth watering in anticipation. However, when the waitress approaches, that amazing meal is being served, not on a pristine dish, but on the lid of a garbage can. Your expectations of that meal have now been completely altered, to say the least. It stands out, but not in a good way. This example might appear extreme, but I wanted to make my point stand out.

When you are trying to brand yourself in a situation, it is important to find ways to stand out, but positively. The reality is that no matter the skills, knowledge, or expertise that you have, without the right presentation, those things are not going to shine. If you don't stand out in a positive way, then you are going into a default mode of blending in, or even worse, standing out in the negative, just like that meal on the garbage lid.

Always look to stand out in some aspect of your dress at any event. A splash of color, special jewelry, shoes, or a hat can help you to stand out. I want you to think about how you can be creative within the parameters of the situation. Fashion shows are all about showcasing creativity, but many of those outfits lack practicality. Yet you can use fashion as inspiration to bring something unique into your daily wardrobe.

I love wearing a fresh pair of Jordan's, and my jogging pants, along with the other aspects that make it my go-to outfit. When it is time to do business, however, I completely adjust my style to present a clean and pressed appearance, which includes a fresh shave, and a suit, tie, and dress shoes. Everything is pressed and neat, reflecting the environment that I am about to enter. Many people have told me that I "clean up so nicely." It is a simple but powerful example of how you need to dress for the situation and environment to create the right presentation.

Therefore, you need to find a way to present yourself, in every situation, in such a way that it does not negatively impact your brand message. Avatars are primarily a way of presenting yourself in any given situation. Spending time analyzing situations, and the message you want to send, can be a great way to determine how best to present yourself and act according to your message.

Think about how you dress for an event. Is it appropriate to the environment? While you have the right to define yourself with body art or piercings, for example, they may not help you stand out positively in every situation. In fact, people often make negative inferences based on appearances, whether it is right or not. If you do not account for that reality, then you are selling yourself short and doing your own career a disservice, just to prove a point. Ultimately, it is up to you to define how you want to present yourself, and then dress the part. Now I agree that appearance should not matter and it's the inside that counts, but the reality of this world is that millisecond you are judged can have rippling impacts on your life. I am not saying you must change every aspect of how you look, I am saying just be conscious and aware of how it will be perceived and be mindful of its impacts.

Now, branding by association is a different kettle of fish, because you are not in control of that perception. Those that you choose to be close associates in your group are going to reflect on how others perceive you. Essentially, your reputation is impacted by their reputations and the perceptions that people have of them.

How often are teenagers lumped together based on their friends? I am here to tell you that everything your mother ever told you about your friends reflecting on you, is true. You're your friends, you are known. Translate that into your career. Who are the top five people that you spend your time with at work? What would people say about you, based on who they are and how they are perceived? The reason is that you are being judged based on how those individuals are judged. If they are seen as lazy and unmotivated, then you are going to be perceived the same way. On the other hand, if they are seen as a driving force in moving the business forward, then you are likely to be judged in the same light.

> *"I tell young entrepreneurs to use the leader in their industry as a benchmark as they work to create their own brand. Don't look at what your competition is doing – if you emulate the leader in your industry, you will achieve a higher level of engagement with consumers and make their buying experience richer."*
> **– Steve Stoute**

Personally, I choose my friends and mentors based on what they are known for and how they are perceived. Present yourself as someone who chooses wisely, and their reputations will positively impact your own, allowing you to take leaps in your career. Surround yourself with like-minded individuals, ones who can help you to push forward and take chances, because they are doing it too.

In college, for example, the party group is known for their drinking, wild nights, and crazy stunts. When you hang out with members of that group, it quickly becomes the perception that people have of you, even if you do none of those things. I don't want to say *guilt by association*, but at times, that is what happens. Birds of a feather flock together. So, if you do not want to be part of their flock, you need to change your feathers!

Think about the individuals that you admire and that inspire you. Then look at who you are spending your time with. Are they doing the things that inspire you to achieve or make real change? Do they hold you accountable? It is so easy to slip into complacency when it comes to who we hang out with at work. The truth is that you can choose to be motivated or you can choose to be brought down. It is up to you!

Additionally, you are going to find that improving your association can lead to greater opportunities, which can catapult you to the next level, or even several levels. Think of it as scaling the walls of your next career goal. Some individuals will help you to scale those walls, giving you encouragement and even practical advice. Others are going to try to sabotage your efforts, even disabling your catapult, so to speak. Therefore, you want to look for those who are willing to help you be successful, not those who want to help you fall backward.

Find the right mix of people that will support you, but also who will reflect well on you and your brand avatar at the same time.

Finally, you need to brand by achievement. It can be great when you win an award, especially if that award holds high honor in your industry. Yet, if that designation or honor means little outside of your current industry, it might not be helpful in terms of furthering your brand outside of your industry. You need to highlight the achievements that will make you stand out to your prospective employers, not achievements that do not make a positive impact on your future goals and prospects.

Think of realtors who put unique designations on their business cards or websites. While they might mean something to another realtor, it means next to nothing for the individual just looking for a realtor to help them sell their house or to buy their next home. They might have been the top realtor for their company, for example, but that translates into very little for their client. What the client wants to know is how fast they typically sell a house, and how satisfied people are that use them for finding their next home. Highlighting achievements that don't tell them what they need to know is not going to help you make the right impression and build a successful brand with your potential clients.

When you look at the honors or awards that you highlight as part of your brand, do they support your message, or do they detract from it, leaving your potential employers or supervisors confused about who you are and what you bring to the table.

Instead, look at your achievements as a chance to showcase your strengths. Depending on the situation, you might highlight a certain award or accomplishment because it demonstrates another ability, skill, or knowledge that you bring to the table. Use your accomplishments to advertise what you are capable of, but remember, it shouldn't be all about your achievements.

Think of your achievements as the icing on the cake of who you are. They might be the first thing that people see, but you want to back them up with something substantial. Every cake has icing that makes it appealing, but what people rave about is the cake itself. Make sure your cake isn't dry and tasteless, being masked by the frosting of your achievements.

How do you build your achievements? Take advantage of tools available through the internet, including webinars, classes, and blogs. I also know there are several professional, but free, options available to give you the chance to grow your knowledge and skill set. If you have teenagers, then you know the power of YouTube. If you go onto the app and start searching, you will quickly see that there is a video tutorial on how to do just about anything! Other options include linda.com, Google, and other industry-oriented sites. The point is to take the time to build those skills and increase your knowledge. It does not have to cost much, but doing so can be a big advantage for you as you look to take leaps in your career.

If you take all of these factors into account as you prepare for different situations, you will start to create consistency in your brand and your message.

Training for Consistency to Create Opportunities

When it comes to any brand message, the importance of consistency cannot be understated. Many brands have suffered, simply because they were not able to keep their brand message consistent across multiple platforms. The confusion created left a negative impression, and if it happens often enough, those negative impressions can eventually destroy a brand.

Your brand needs to be consistent, because if it isn't, then you will not be able to make the moves necessary to take the giant leaps you want in your career.

> *"An authentic and honest brand narrative is fundamental today;*
> *otherwise, you will simply be edited out."*
> **– Marco Bizzarri**

First, I want you to think about all the opportunities you have throughout the day to brand yourself and communicate your brand message. It could be meetings, social gatherings of workmates, or even how you execute various projects and assignments. Each of these is a moment where you communicate who you are and what you represent. You can either stand out or you can blend in. The choice is up to you. Are you muddying the waters for yourself by a lack of consistency?

For instance, you might have expressed an interest to expand your skills by taking on other projects outside of your current job description. When those opportunities arise, do you take them seriously and give it your all? Do the people you work with see your willingness to get it done, and that you are asking for help if needed? Are you presenting a message that compliments the team player brand message you want to create, or are others finding it difficult to work with you? Once you start building a reputation or perception from one project to another, it can be very difficult to alter that message. Again, a lack of consistency can negatively impact your brand!

Coca-Cola is an example of how inconsistency can damage your brand. In the mid-1970s, Pepsi decided to do a brand challenge with Coke. In taste comparisons, Coke was losing to Pepsi. The brand countered with New Coke, which was a better formulation. Once they saw that New Coke was doing well, the company announced that it would phase out the old Coke formula, and New Coke would be the brand's main offering going forward. Even though it was clearly a better product, protests abounded, as the original was what the customers wanted. In the end, Coke brought back the original formula as Classic Coke. The New Coke formula eventually faded away. Recognizable brands are known for being dependable, and as Coke learned, the actual quality of the product can often take a back seat to the consistency of the brand and its products.

When you are consistent though, the messaging comes through clear and on point. Time and again, that on point messaging can be the key that opens those doors of opportunity. Are you giving yourself the chance to reap those opportunities, or are you essentially shooting yourself in the proverbial foot?

On the other hand, Apple has created a successful brand that is consistent in testing limits and being innovative. That is what its customers expect. When Apple Music started, the brand wanted to give customers a 3-month free trial to build demand for the product. The problem was that they also didn't want to pay royalties to the artists during that time. The issue of royalties prompted letters from various artists, most notably Taylor Swift. Apple quickly changed their position and paid royalties during that time period. The artists responded by promoting Apple Music, a product that continues to grow.

The point was that Apple listened to all the stakeholders, and made adjustments that were consistent with their brand. In the end, Apple has remained consistent in its branding, and that has shown in the results of the company.

I love to watch successful businesses and people brand themselves consistently. No matter where they are communicating their message, you are getting the same message or variations of the same message.

It is constant and supports the brand. On the other hand, those that are not successful put their brand message out there in a way that leaves people feeling frustrated and confused. No matter how long I work in branding, the fact is that people make this mistake over and over again, because they do not maintain the consistency in their message.

If you are leaving individuals feeling confused, especially prospective employers, then they are not likely to turn to you and give you those opportunities that you are actively craving to make the leaps that will help you achieve your goals and fulfill your purpose.

"Define what your brand stands for, its core values and tone of voice, and then communicate consistently in those terms."
– Simon Mainwaring

Still, it can be hard to have a consistent message for your brand, if you do not take the time to figure out what that message is going to be. So, how can you define your message in order to create consistency? It starts with your vision and finding your voice.

Creating Your Voice and Vision

Right now, I want you to stop and think about your goals. Where do you see yourself in one year, five years, or even ten years? Those goals will define your purpose and help you to find your vision and the voice that matches that vision.

"It's very important for a brand to have an identity through the years, but it's very important as well to evolve because times change so fast."
– Donatella Versace

Those goals are going to give you a framework for your vision, but keep in mind, you are going to evolve as time goes on. That means your brand needs to evolve as well. Consistent messaging allows you to keep the foundation of your brand the same while altering aspects of your message to reflect how you have evolved and changed.

Potential employers do not want individuals who are not willing to learn and grow. They want to be able to tap into new skills, and into knowledge and experience, they do not currently have. When you show your ability to adapt, change, and thrive, as part of your brand's evolution, then you are sending the message that you will bring that to their business, tapping into their needs.

As part of defining your vision of where you want to go, you need to define your goals and timeframe for reaching them. Once you have determined what you want to achieve, then you need to craft your message to reflect your goals. Your brand is going to be defined by that message. Your goals are the outward sign of your vision.

Why is it so important to have a vision? Think of a boat without a rudder. It goes where the ocean or lake's waves direct it. There is no direction and without direction, who knows where the boat will end up. I want you to recognize that the point of having a vision is to give yourself direction. You need to put yourself in control. Otherwise, events and circumstances can toss you in a direction that you did not want to go.

How do you create a vision? You need to start with three key components:

- Your values
- Your future goals
- Your life's purpose

All of them will play a part in the creation of your vision and where you want to take your career.

Think of it this way. Your purpose is the "why" or reason you are going down a certain path or setting specific goals. It is the reason behind your actions and efforts. Your purpose inspires change. When it comes to your vision, you are creating the "what" that you want to accomplish as a result of the "why." When you are committed to your purpose, then your vision becomes easier to define. Finally, your mission is the actual steps that you take to achieve the vision—essentially, the "how."

Therefore, the first thing that you need to do is to define your purpose or your why. You might know that you want to move forward in your career, but the question is, why do you want to do that? It should play into the larger goal of the life that you want. Do not confuse your purpose with your goals or the strategies to achieve your goals. Your purpose is a guiding light that inspires you and guides the choices you make and the goals that you set.

Now, let's talk about creating a vision. Since it is the "what," it is going to be more in-depth than your purpose, but it is critical because, without your vision, you cannot set out the "how," or create a timeframe to achieve those goals.

Here are seven key ways to create a vision for yourself:

1. **Define Your Purpose for Your Career** – What are you working toward? You can have a vision about multiple areas of your life, so it is important to be clear about what you are working toward in your career. You might be working toward management, or you might be working toward early retirement. You could be looking for your exit strategy, regarding your own business or to move into another company, or you could be considering a career shift. Your purpose might be a position that allows you to impact the community or a specific group of people positively. If you don't know your purpose, it can be hard to create a vision of what you want to achieve.

2. **Define Your Timeframe** – No one has ever successfully envisioned their future and made it happen without creating a timeframe. Without deadlines, your vision will simply remain a dream, and your career will not move forward in the direction that you want it to go. At the same time, make sure that it is a realistic timeframe. Putting things too far out, you end up with no sense of urgency, and that means little motivation to take risks and jump on those opportunities. Choosing short and long-term goals can keep you motivated, while still working toward larger achievements.

3. **Don't Ignore Past Achievements** – You are going to need encouragement as you move forward. By making a list of past achievements, you can focus on how good it felt to achieve those goals. It creates a base of positivity and energy that you can use to build future successes. When you focus on the positive, you are likely to achieve the greatness that you have already envisioned.

4. **Draft a Vision** – It can be easy to limit yourself in terms of what you want in your vision. As you write this draft, be sure to include everything that you want, no matter how crazy it might seem to be. Build your passions into what you write. Your vision needs to represent you because if you are not focusing on your passions, it can be hard to keep yourself motivated and excited about your vision. Make sure that it is written down and accessible to you visually on a daily basis. Take advantage of sticky notes, tacks, and a cork board, or even tape and a dry erase board. Remember, the point is that you need to be able to change and update it, so make sure you can add and remove things as needed.

5. **Review, Draft, Repeat** – As you revise, ask yourself if it is inspiring and exciting, or do you find it boring, off-putting, or even vague? Revision time is when you get clearer and more specific, but also when you put real concrete information into your vision. Once you revise, read it again, and continue to adjust until you have a solid draft. Still, do not get so focused on creating the draft of your vision

that you paralyze yourself from moving forward. Instead, after about four revisions, consider it ready for the next step.

6. **Solicit Input** – Turn to people you trust and respect; in particular, those leaders that you want to be part of your associates (remember, brand by association). They might also focus on the action steps you need to take to achieve that vision. Keep those thoughts handy, as they will help you later, but in the meantime, use their input to make additional adjustments to your vision statement.

7. **Share Your Vision** – At this point, you have a vision statement, and now it is time to share that vision using your brand avatar. You might also find individuals asking you how you plan to achieve that vision, but that is a focus on the "how," and at this moment, you are focused more on the vision, which is the "what."

Now that you have a vision, you need to follow through in communicating that vision to yourself and others in an effective way. Speak your vision verbally and constantly think about it consciously and continuously. Bombard your brain and body with your vision daily to make it part of the fabric of you (inside and out).

Wrap Up for Chapter 2 (Get Set to Adjust Your Mindset)

- Branding needs to be consistent.
- Be aware of the perceptions that you create in:
  - Appearance
  - Association
  - Achievement
- Use a vision board to understand where you are going, and to help you understand what you stand for as a brand.

Still, to achieve any vision, you need to have a plan, or a map, that you can follow to attain the results you want, and be able to measure your progress in light of various challenges. In *setting your objectives for success*, I am going to help you define your objectives and create a plan to achieve your career goals. In this chapter, I will focus on how to define your goals and create a plan and timeline to achieve those goals, which will help you stay on track in reaching your objectives.

Chapter 3

Setting Your Objectives for Success

"If you want to be happy, set a goal that commands your thoughts, liberates your energy, and inspires your hopes."
– Andrew Carnegie

What you will learn:

- To define your goals – which are the markers of your life course.
- To create a plan – one that gives you a timeline for achieving those goals.

No matter where you are in your career, you know that in order to determine your progress, you need to have defined ways of measuring it. Without an objective measurement, it is impossible to know if you are reaching your objectives, or if your efforts are contributing to your progress.

In many ways, the efforts that you put into your branding, and into the creation of your brand avatar, may all be a waste if you do not have a way to determine if you are making progress. Let's start by talking about your vision again. It is where you want to go, and the picture of the life that you want to live. Part of that vision is what you want to ultimately achieve with your brand and in terms of your career.

Therefore, let's start by discussing the importance of goals, especially your ultimate ones.

"You have to understand your own personal DNA. Don't do things because I do them or Steve Jobs or Mark Cuban tried it. You need to know your personal brand and stay true to it."
– Gary Vaynerchuk

Define Your Ultimate Goals

When you plan the course of your career, you make it clear that you want to achieve a certain result. Therefore, you create your goals with that end in mind. In the last chapter, I talked about vision. Goals, on the other hand, are all the things you will do to accomplish that overarching vision. All the goals you set for yourself are part of a larger plan to allow you to reach the end of your path. When it comes to your career, you might have a result in mind, but opportunities that present themselves take you on another path entirely. It does not mean that you do not have goals or objectives on this new path, but they may no longer match your previous ones.

My point is that ultimate goals should mark your career. These are goals that stand the test of time; ones tied to your purpose and what you want to achieve in life overall. Think of an ultimate goal as one that has to do with the legacy you leave behind for others.

In the business world, you might serve as a mentor, helping others to achieve in their career paths. Regardless of what company you work for, or the business that you might create, that goal of mentoring would still be viable. Essentially, your ultimate goal is to help others on the path to achieving their goals and dreams, by mentoring them with your experiences, skills, and knowledge.

"Any entrepreneur worth their salt knows that their brand is worthless if it doesn't somehow contribute to society or the overall good of the planet."
– Lynda Resnick

Do you see my point? Your ultimate goals are greater than just one particular job or one particular career path. When you choose your ultimate goals, you are defining your course based on specific long-term expectations of what you want to be, and the impact you want to have.

Start by listing what you want to be remembered for after you are gone. If you think about it that way, you begin to define what you want to achieve in your life and the legacy that you want to leave behind.

Also, look at what brings you joy and gets you excited to get out of bed in the morning. These are the things that can help you to define your purpose in the world. What you want to achieve in your life is often directly related to what your purpose is and what gives you a sense of joy. Your legacy is wrapped up in that purpose, which needs to be greater than just you, involving how you can give back to others.

All of these aspects are going to be part of the brand avatar that you create because the message and actions of your brand avatar are based on meeting those ultimate goals. The point of your brand is to help you make the leaps in your career that are going to get you to the next level, and that much closer to achieving your ultimate goals.

Within those ultimate goals are going to be smaller goals, the ones that help you to achieve your ultimate goals. The question is how to identify those smaller goals, and what type of plan you need to create to achieve those goals.

Create a Plan to Achieve Your Goals

Your ultimate goals are going to be the guideposts to achieving your purpose and the vision you have for your life and career. To do so, it helps to break down a larger goal into smaller ones. Once you have your smaller goals, it is important to put an action plan in place to help you achieve them and to hold yourself accountable for the results. It is important that your action plan includes a timeframe for achieving those goals.

When you decide you want to change a habit, for example, you might put together a plan, but without a defined timeframe, you can go weeks, months, or even years without making any progress in achieving that goal. I know that without a timeframe to hold you accountable, life can distract you, leaving you feeling defeated and frustrated because you have not achieved what you had hoped to before a certain time in your life.

Your career goals need to have that same timeframe and determination attached to them. Time after time, I find that people who set a timeframe for their goals are more successful, simply because they hold themselves accountable for making progress. In your career, if you want to make the kinds of leaps that will help you achieve phenomenal growth, then you need to have an action plan. Without it, you will not make the kind of forward progress necessary to achieve everything that is possible in your life.

Your action plan needs to include the following:

- **The ultimate goal** – Define the largest goal. Give details, and make it clear what you want to achieve.
- **Steps to achieve that ultimate goal** – As you detail the ultimate goal, there will be some clear steps that you can use to define the path to that goal. Make a list of those items, as they will become the steps that you need to achieve it.

- **Create an action plan** – Take the steps that you have defined, and put them into the order that will help you achieve them sooner. Some steps might rely on others, so be sure to keep them in order.
- **Network, network, network** – As part of your action plan, it is important to identify those who can help you to achieve your objectives. Then, make a point to create those connections.
- **Create a timeframe** – The point of your timeframe is to hold you accountable for acting on your action plan and achieving the smaller steps that you outlined. Without a timeframe, it is easy to lose your focus.

Now that you have a plan, one that gets you excited because you can see how to achieve your ultimate goals, it is time to look for role models—those who have been successful. Why?

Practicing Activities of Successful People

You have a plan to achieve your ultimate goals, but you need to recognize that you are going to have to deal with various obstacles along your path. Finding role models and practicing the activities that they practice to be successful can help you to overcome those obstacles. At the same time, you are creating a set of habits that can help you to overcome any situation but also to propel you forward.

Choosing the right people to model means looking at what they have achieved and how they did it. Essentially, you are allowing them to mentor you from afar, and using their experiences as inspiration to propel you forward. So many times, reading about the experiences of another individual, who has already trod the path you want to take, can give you clues about what you might experience, and what challenges you might face. You can also learn what they did to overcome those obstacles and challenges; essentially, what inspires them and gives them strength to move forward.

How do you choose your mentors? For me, it is about reading, listening to webinars, and talking with others about who inspired them. Doing so can lead you to the people that will give you the benefits of their wisdom, experience, and perspectives, through their books or talks. However, to have a mentor that will hold you accountable, you need to find someone that you can personally reach out to and talk with regularly.

To connect with someone, look around at the people you already know and work with regularly. Is there someone that you are inspired by? Are they already where you want to be? Start finding ways to work with them, adding to conversations they have started. Show that you appreciate what they do and are open to learning from them. You also want to be someone who is open to being mentored. Show that you are open to making changes, are working hard to improve on your own, and are participating at the highest level possible right now. Mentors tend to find those who are demonstrating that they are willing to learn.

There are also opportunities to find mentors through online mentoring networks, networking events, and industry meet-ups. Use these opportunities to build your network, and then reach out to members of that network from time to time. Share what you are working on, and be willing to ask questions about how they took their career to the next level. You will be amazed at how the mentoring relationship can flow from there.

Finally, there are also paid mentorships, which allow you to make a connection, and then have regular meetings with your mentor, to help you achieve your goals and give you a constructive perspective on how you might be standing in your own way. Think of it as a therapy for your career, although mentors can also be helpful in keeping you on the path to achieving your personal goals as well.

It is often not a question of asking someone to mentor you, as it is demonstrating that you are willing to be mentored. Those who you want to be mentored by are busy in their own right, so they are looking to give their time to those who aren't going to waste time but use what they offer and will take action on the information that is presented. The point is that everyone has to learn from somebody else, either through defined lessons in a paid mentorship or through informal interactions. Unless you already have experience, then you owe it to your career to find people who can broaden your perspective and illuminate details that you might have otherwise missed.

Additionally, those you may want to serve as mentors are often very successful , usually in an area where you might be personally struggling. I have found that those whose success I want to emulate consistently appear to be doing several key things that you can also apply to achieve your ultimate goals.

Time Management – Time is a commodity that we all have, but how often do we manage it effectively? I want to be clear here that time management is not about scheduling your day to get the maximum number of activities in during the day, but about delegating activities so that you can focus on what inspires you and what brings you joy, and the fulfillment of your purpose.

Start by making a list of all the activities you do on a daily basis. Which of those activities do you really enjoy, and which ones do you put off because you don't enjoy them, or they do not help move you forward to your purpose? I find that delegation is key, because it allows you to take those tasks that you do not enjoy, and give them to someone else. It could mean that you hire a personal assistant, a housekeeper, or even just have better delegation of tasks at your job. Doing so will give you more time for the things you enjoy about your job, and will allow you to demonstrate leadership. Plus, when you are delegating, you are freeing yourself up to meet key deadlines, because you are freeing yourself from the activities that suck up your time.

Additionally, take advantage of the time management tools available, such as calendar apps or daily planner reminders. In this day and age, you can have calendar apps for all aspects of your life. Gone are the days of the paper day-planner, a book that became the successful person's *Bible*. If it was lost, you panicked, because it meant that you no longer knew where you were supposed to be or who you were meeting with! Instead, your phone, computer, and tablet can all be synced to allow you to access your calendar in the office or on the go. The daily planner couldn't remind you of events or tasks, so you had to check it frequently. If your staff was keeping that book for you, there was always the chance of error, because you could both be making appointments for the same period. There was no such thing as syncing those daily planner books. Technology, however, has given us the ability to not only sync our calendars, but also to share events, invite others, and have constant reminders to keep us on task. Your calendar can also be divided into family events, work events, and personal events. Everything can be accounted for in one place, instead of all over! Take advantage of the technological tools, and find what works for you!

Eating Right/Exercising – If you are trying to reach some major goals, you are going to need energy and stamina to stay on the path. Your body is the factory that will produce that energy and stamina, but only if you take care of it. Successful people practice self-care, and that includes eating well to give their bodies the fuel needed to move them forward. When you don't take care of yourself, you eat up your body's reserves and, eventually, you will run out of gas. That moment could be one where you have an amazing opportunity, but you are unable to take advantage of it due to having run yourself into the ground.

Granted, not all of us find exercise fun. Some of you might think that exercise is more akin to a special brand of torture than an enjoyable activity. Before you dismiss it, though, start exploring the different options out there. No matter if you are coordinated, or falling in the realm of the klutzes, there is an exercise option out there for you. It is just a matter of trying different options and finding the one you enjoy the most.

It can be easy to eat unhealthy food options and waste your financial resources when you are on the go throughout the day. Taking the time to plan your week, and prep healthy snacks to take along with you daily is key to keeping you on track regarding healthy eating. If you already have your snacks and lunch with you, there is less temptation to spend resources on unhealthy options. Picking a day, such as Sunday afternoon, can allow you to organize your meals and snacks for the week. The benefit is that you don't have to think about what's for lunch; you can just grab it and go!

Exercising is another aspect of this self-care that you cannot neglect. When you move, you allow hormones and endorphins to do the work needed to keep you pumped up and excited. It is critical that you take the time to do this for yourself. When your body is well cared for, you can be successful. Additionally, by taking the time to care for yourself, you give your mind a chance to meditate and take a break. Doing so can allow the ideas and inspiration to flow. Practicing self-care allows successful people to achieve all that they want and more, simply because they are energized to take on the challenges in front of them.

Here is another opportunity to tap into technology. Your phone or other electronic devices can give you access to apps where you can set fitness goals and even track the number of steps you take daily. Use them to remind you to get up and walk throughout your day. Add small changes to your routine that force you to walk or just get up and move. Walk or pace your office while on the phone. Park your car further out to require you to walk more in the morning and the evening. Take the stairs versus the elevator. Little behavioral shifts can result in big changes! It is important to make these small changes, but also important to track your progress. Once you achieve one goal, set another. The point is to keep you focused on moving throughout your day, and keeping your body healthy as a result.

In the matrix below, I want to get you thinking about how you fill your days. Everything you do falls into one of these categories. The point is to place everything into the different boxes, and then allow that to prioritize your day. For example, a task that lands in boxes 1 (Urgent/Important) and 2 (Not Urgent/Important) should be given priority over tasks that fall into boxes 3 (Urgent/Unimportant) and 4 (Not Urgent/Unimportant).

Urgent/Important	Not Urgent/Important
Urgent/Unimportant	Not Urgent/Unimportant

These are just two practices of successful people. One of the most successful motivational coaches in the world, Stephen Covey, wrote a book that propelled his message into the international spotlight. In his book, *The 7 Habits of Highly Effective People*, Covey laid out the seven principles for success. As he studied successful people, he noted that they all do the same things consistently, and he recognized that for others to be successful, they needed to practice these things as well. Here are a few of those habits, and how they can help you to move forward in your career.

Taking the Initiative – In your career, to be successful in creating real growth, you need to be willing to put yourself out there. It does not mean being pushy, but making yourself available, even volunteering to take on projects that might be more challenging. Doing so will allow you to set yourself apart from the rest, giving you the advantage when it comes to promotions or other opportunities.

Put First Things First – When you create a clear understanding of what needs to be done, focus in on the results, not the methods used to get there. Be willing to be creative and keep your focus on what you want to accomplish. Focus on the top priorities but remember that does not always mean urgent. When you are focused on those priorities, then you are not going to be wasting energy on tasks that distract you from your goals.

Understand Others First Before You Try to be Understood – When you seek to understand others first, then you are shifting the paradigm of how you listen. Most of us are guilty of listening to reply, instead of listening to understand. You find that those individuals are preparing to speak, or are already in the process of speaking. That is essentially only half of the communication process, meaning that if you are not listening to understand another individual, then you are missing out on half of the conversation.

Develop a Winning Frame of Mind – This frame of mind focuses on seeking the mutual benefits of everyone, in all your interactions. It is not the same as compromise, because compromising means that someone wins, and someone will lose by default. Aiming to give everyone an outcome, where they are content and happy, means that you are creating a setting where people can work together instead of against each other. In a business setting, your bosses will find this a key leadership skill, because you will be able to work with your team to help them be successful.

The point of all these habits is to create action and forward motion as you work to achieve your ultimate goals. Be proactive in your journey to create real change in your life and your career. Your smaller goals need to be prioritized to help you move through them quickly and effectively.

Here are some questions to ask yourself as you look for successful people to use as examples and inspiration in a variety of circumstances. These questions focus on your actions, but you can also answer them using the actions of a successful individual you admire. It can help you to dissect what they are doing right, and how you can imitate that in your own career.

- Have you achieved a win-win situation, instead of a compromise? What made it successful, and what can you repeat the next time?
- Can you think of key moments where you seek to understand the other person, listening without thinking about your response? What skills can you develop to improve your ability to understand others?
- How do you push yourself through the worst times?
- What gets you motivated?
- What keeps you awake at night? What are you afraid of, and is it keeping you from doing what you know you need to do?
- What are your strengths? How can you maximize your strengths?
- What decisions can you stop making? What can you make routine to preserve your energy for more important things?
- What hard (or difficult) thing are you not doing enough of? Can you reframe it so that you focus more on why the task is important, versus focusing on the task itself?
- What easy things are you doing that are keeping you from tackling those harder tasks?
- How are you going to implement the changes that need to be made?

It is important to note that part of any process of creating goals and your action plan is acknowledging that you might fall down. There are also habits that you might not have but that will be necessary for you to be successful. Renew yourself by focusing on gaining those habits. Doing so will help you to move forward to achieving your action plan, and to making a successful jump in your career.

The Benefits of Vision Boards and Affirmations

When you created your vision, I pointed out how important it is to have a physical representation of that vision. Using a vision board, you can give your vision life and use it as inspiration to move yourself forward to achieve your goals. Visualization works, and it can help you to make progress, as well as to improve your performance. Just ask Olympic athletes, who have been using visualization for decades to improve their performances in their various sports. With these benefits in mind, how can you make a vision board?

First, your vision board should focus on how you want to feel, and not just on the things that you want to achieve.

Start by adding things to your board that remind you of specific feelings or experiences that inspired you. It could be a moment you were happy or one where you felt accomplished, or even a moment where you knew you looked fantastic, and it was a confidence booster. These items serve as reminders, so that every time you see them, your brain remembers that feeling as well.

It can also include things that you want to keep happening regularly, such as photos from annual vacations or a gala award dinner. Quotes that inspire you, or reminders, can round out your board.

Change things out as you find new inspiration, or rearrange as necessary. Don't feel that you have to stay locked into your original vision board as things change in your life. Consider clearing your board in December and starting fresh, allowing you to focus on the new year and what you want to accomplish.

What do you need for a vision board? Choose a type of board that appeals to you. Use scissors, tape, pins, or even a glue-stick to put your board together. Magazines can be a source of images, but also include the stuff that you want to look at every day. Don't rush the process, but take a chunk of time to create it. Then, allow it to evolve throughout the year. During the initial stage of creation, set the mood, making it a stress-free period.

The purpose of the board is to bring your focus to life. Whatever you focus on tends to expand, and you will be amazed at how things start to pop up once you set your intention regarding how you want to feel and what you want to accomplish. You can have one large vision board or several small ones. Make sure that's front and center in your daily routine so that you can focus on it regularly.

Additionally, you can create affirmations. When you affirm something, you are stating that it is true. They are dynamic and powerful. To get the best results from your affirmations, be sure to repeat them daily and give yourself a quiet space to concentrate in.

I know individuals that find meditation, in the morning, where they focus on their affirmations, to be a great start to their day. Others prefer the evening, right before bed, to do their affirmations and allow their mind to quiet after a busy day. Do what works for you, but just remember to make a place for this time daily.

All of these methods are beneficial because they help you to focus in on what you need to do to achieve your ultimate goals and purpose. Do not be afraid to use these tools to help you stick to your action plan. Remember that the point of everything you are doing is about propelling yourself to the next level in the fastest way possible. It is inspiring when you keep yourself on the path and start to see the payoff.

Wrap Up for Chapter 3 (Setting Your Objectives for Success)

- It is key to define your ultimate goals and to create a plan to achieve them.
- Use vision boards and affirmations to help you stay focused on your goals and being successful in creating the life that you want.
- Imitate the habits of successful people in order to be successful in your own life.

Part of obtaining the success that you want is walking a fine line between doing what is necessary to be successful and knowing when to draw the line to avoid selling out on who you are. In the next chapter, *When to Blend In and When to Stand Out*, I will focus on how you can use your brand avatar to step out of your comfort zone, to understand the difference between selling out and blending into your environment, as well as the importance of taking a hard stand, which will help you to stand out at your company and in your industry.

Chapter 4

When to Blend in and When to Stand Out

"Without differentiation, you have no brand."
– Bernard Kelvin Clive

What you will learn in this chapter:

* Knowing when to do what you are not comfortable with
* Understanding the difference between selling out and blending into your environment
* When to take a hard stance, acknowledging that it isn't your thing

Selling out has gotten a bad rap over the years. Often associated with brownnosing, going against what you should do to get ahead or kissing up. The idea implies doing whatever it takes to get ahead, even if it crosses ethical, cultural or moral lines. In the world of business, the idea of "I'll scratch your back, if you scratch mine," is part of how things get done at times. Appearances are important, but the question of why you are behaving a certain way is even more critical. After all, people might not know the reason, and they may question your actions, and even call you a sellout.

The lemming mentality is often associated with brownnosing, simply because it revolves around the idea of following the crowd, without any individual thought processes of your own. There is a difference between following the crowd with an understanding of why you are doing so, versus doing it simply because you see others doing it. You need to become more conscious of "why" you are doing certain things, instead of just going along.

Within those moments, you have to decide between whether it is truly selling out in the negative sense, or if you are actually doing what is necessary to get to the next step.

When you build your brand avatar, it is meant to influence others to offer you opportunities that allow you to make those leaps in your career that will take you where you want to go.

Think about all the brands that are part of your life, from the moment you wake up in the morning. There are ads which market products and services for you to use, buy, or even promote to your own family and friends. It can be easy for you to stop being consciously aware of how all these marketing techniques influence you. They are building a brand with you as their target audience, and are influencing your decisions in the process.

Using your brand avatar, you can take advantage of opportunities, making choices and doing things with the end in mind. Others might see you as brownnosing, because you are quick to volunteer for a project, or are subtler when voicing your opinion or ideas to certain individuals in charge. The reality is that you are willing to do what needs to be done to get ahead.

High school is a great example of this process. During those years, there were crowds and cliques. Depending on who you hung out with, you might be expected to participate in certain activities or act a specific way. The cool kids might make a point not to associate with different kids, and it was possible that to stay in that crowd, you were not kind to those kids. You wanted to do what was expected of you to keep your position, even though it might not have been true to who you were as an individual. Essentially, you create an avatar to get through being a teenager. Your career is no different.

Professionally, you may also find yourself stepping outside of your comfort zone to do things that you might be hesitant about taking on. I want you to understand that to advance in your career, you are going to be uncomfortable. You need to be willing to stretch yourself, recognizing that opportunities do not come your way if you are not open to risk.

> *"It's up to you to define your own brand of leadership and your own version of success."*
> **– Peggy Johnson**

I want you to be open to standing out as well. It might be easy to do the work behind the scenes, but not receive the credit. Blending in allows you to learn the environment, better understand the needs of those in charge, and then help you to find ways to address those needs, allowing you to stand out.

Within the realm of business, you need to recognize that who you are in the office reflects your career and where you want to go. Therefore, your brand avatar should be the means you use to step outside of your comfort zone while helping you to better understand the professional environment of your department, your company, and your industry.

Never Forget Where You Came From

That phrase is often quoted and individuals, who have been successful, credit their longevity in their business with their ability to "remember where they came from," and to "never change." As a human being, you are always growing, learning, and changing in terms of your skills and knowledge base. The idea that you will never change is really not accurate. However, what shouldn't change are the fundamentals of who you are as a person, as a business owner, as an employee, or as an entrepreneur.

You become known for specific actions, a way of behaving, and a method of doing business that becomes associated with who you are. Many of the ways that you choose to behave start with where you were raised, the values you were raised with, and the experiences you had. Where you came from is a powerful place, because it helped to shape who you are and what you became. That background either gave you the fuel to succeed, or it made you complacent. If you came from an environment to the contrary, you can still win by being conscious of various forms of negative programming that plague the environment and not make it be a part of your consciousness. I know, easier said than done, but through constant and continuous positive reinforcement, backed by actionable activities that align with where you want to be, you will get there.

All of us have a story based on where we came from and how it altered us. Think about your childhood. Was there a particularly powerful moment that stands out for you? I have heard individuals talk about moments with their parents when they saw them stand up for what was right, or break down under pressure, making choices that ran contrary to who they were.

> *"Regardless of age, regardless of position, regardless of the business we happen to be in, all of us need to understand the importance of branding. We are CEOs of our own companies: Me, Inc. To be in business today, our most important job is to be head marketer for the brand called You."*
> **– Tom Peters**

Building a brand does not have to mean selling some fake version of yourself to appeal to others. It is about identifying the best version of who you are and then breathing life into that version, giving people something to connect with.

I read an interesting story of a brand marketer, author, and blogger, Celinne Da Costa, who used to feel that *personal branding* was part of fabricating a specific image, even if that image had no basis in reality, and then using that image to convince others to make purchasing choices.

Then she went on a journey, using her social media following to find hosts for her trip around the world. She admitted that the locals needed to know who she was so that they could be comfortable with bringing her into their families and homes. Her personal brand became one focused on communicating who she was and what her purpose was for the journey and then giving her audience a "why," to help them to tie the pieces together.

At the end of her journey, she had a much different perspective of personal branding. "Your personal brand is not just what you say you are: it is an accumulation of what you do," said Da Costa. Her advice: find a way to connect with your audience, and do it with integrity.

When you take where you came from, and use it as a base to connect with others, then it truly becomes a way for them to want to work with you. In these moments, you are not pretending to be something; you are demonstrating who you are. From a professional standpoint, being true to your roots and who you are is the best way to build a brand of integrity that individuals will count on.

Do you have a story, one that is unique to you? The reality is that unlike a company, you are an individual, and you have a story to tell, one that is yours alone. A strong personal brand can move your career forward, but it can also help you to resonate with your audience and move them to action. In this case, the result could be moving your boss to take a leap and give you the next big project or promotion.

You might also find yourself in a position to mentor someone else, and move them to act in a way that helps boost their career. You need to see yourself and your story as critical to communicating who you are to others, and it will help them to believe in you and what you are capable of producing. You may find that you strike an emotional chord with others, and you shouldn't see that as a weakness. Emotional connections give others a reason to feel invested in who you are and what you want to accomplish.

"The only thing I know is I ain't changing my brand. I know what I believe. I'm confident in what I know, and I'm gonna say it. And if folks like it, wonderful. If they don't like it, I understand."
– Joe Biden, former U.S. Vice President

At this point, I want to let you in on a secret. If you are branding yourself solely to gain followers in social media, or to make a specific impression on a boss, then it is not going to work for the long-term. The reality is that influence is often more about quality than quantity. It can feel like a numbers game, but that numbers game is only effective if you are creating meaningful connections that are moving others to act.

What works for you, based on who you are and where you came from, is going to vary from person to person. I can't tell you that what works for me personally will exactly fit your brand avatar. The point is to find what works for you and then use it to build the attention and influence you need to grow your career in a major way. Practice what you preach, and the rest will follow.

At the same time, be a curator of your story. It can be so easy to overshare, to the point that you have drowned out the important details in a sea of information. You have someone at your office that talks constantly: they tell you everything they did over the weekend; they share all the tidbits of their family's drama; and they seem to overshare about virtually everything. How frustrating is that when it comes time to get down to work, and they are drowning you in unnecessary information?

I want you to recognize that blending in or standing out is about planning, to a degree, what you want to be part of your brand avatar, and then promoting that as it supports your vision. Recognize that you can start the process by sharing your knowledge, expertise, and insights. You can and will evolve, but the point is that the core of who you are is based on where you came from and what you want to accomplish.

Standing out happens when you step out of your comfort zone and speak out. For instance, you might have an idea that could positively impact production, but you are not comfortable speaking up during meetings. By using your brand avatar to speak up, you are stepping outside of that comfort zone, but also getting the recognition that you deserve. Keeping your head down and doing your work might be effective in the short run, but taking dramatic leaps in your career means standing out and making a good impression on those in your department and your company. Eventually, that turns into a reputation that filters into your industry.

The point is that balancing blending in and standing out often means recognizing when it is beneficial to step outside of your comfort zone, and when it is better to blend in. Learning the ropes of a department might mean blending in and getting the lay of the land. Over time, you might start standing out more, allowing your ideas and work to showcase what you bring to the table.

I can think of several areas where that balance comes into play. Think about when a company is getting ready to expand. They are looking for leaders and may have a policy of promoting from within. Now is the time for your skills and experience to stand out, by letting your reputation and body of work speak for you. During downsizing, you might find blending in a better fit, as you want to not stand out as someone who is difficult to work with or that struggles to get things done in a timely fashion.

That being said, there are plenty of individuals who get where they want in their careers but do not take the time to reach back and help others. Their reputation is one of ruthlessness in business. People fear them but may have little respect for them. When they run into difficulties, their bridges may have all been burnt. When you have an attitude of gratitude, one where people who work with you feel appreciated, then your brand avatar gives you another way to stand out.

Always Have an Attitude of Gratitude

In this day and age, having an attitude of gratitude is key to connecting with others and recognizing how we are all tied together. No one operates in a vacuum. When you express gratitude to others, you recognize how they have contributed to who you are, what you have accomplished, and even perhaps how they influenced the course that you are on now.

Gratitude also keeps you humble and allows you to see how far you have come, and how much work was involved. It helps you to acknowledge your mentors and those in your network that were part of what drove you forward.

When you are genuinely grateful, it builds your reputation. People appreciate being thanked for the assistance that they give, and for being acknowledged for how they have impacted your life. Networking events are a great time to stand out for your gratitude. Thank people for their contact information, and then take the time to send them a follow-up email, thanking them for their time and their conversation. You are standing out while building new relationships through actions that individuals will come to associate with you and your brand avatar.

I know that hiring managers often remember those interviewees who take the time to thank them for the interview and even thank them for their time after the decision is made. Not all the decisions are favorable, but that attitude of gratitude reflects well on you. Who knows how that make come back to assist you later?

Plus, when you say thank you, it shows other qualities to those in your network and potential employers. It shows that you are conscientious, that you take the time to follow up, and that you are serious about doing things well. So often, we can fail to realize how those moments of saying thank you impact the perception people have of us.

An attitude of gratitude also helps you to connect with who you are and keep you grounded. It can be easy to get a big head, but that big head can often lead to a big fall, as you step away from what makes you unique to your employers, co-workers, and others in the industry.

Evolving means that you take advantage of learning from others, including your mentors. With an attitude of gratitude, you can take that information, put it to use, and give credit to those that helped you along the way. You stand out in a positive and more meaningful way.

Do not put yourself in a situation where you regret where you have been or that you are unable to follow your path because you boxed yourself in. Step out of your comfort zone, allowing your brand avatar to work for you. After a while, it will become natural and will help you to make the best choices for your career to blast off.

Wrap Up for Chapter 4 (When to Blend in and When to Stand Out)

- Blend in to learn about the environment and the connections, but don't be afraid to stand out by stepping outside of your comfort zone.
- Remember, your brand is telling a unique story, the story of you! Let that story be heard, and don't make it like everyone else's.
- Have an attitude of gratitude, and you will be able to find the joy in all areas of your life.

Throughout these chapters, I spent a lot of time focusing in on you, who you are, and understanding where you want to go. Now I want to focus in on your environment, and how that impacts your brand avatar and the choices you need to make to be effective in creating those blasts forward in your career!

For any avatar to be successful, however, it is important to have an *understanding of your environment.* In this chapter, I am going to focus on learning about the environment of your industry and company; how standards can impact your work; finding a way to be productive, instead of just active; and how to stand out in a crowd, which will help you to maximize the benefits of your environment.

Part 2

Creating Your Ideal Universe
Where You Win

Chapter 5

Understanding Your Environment

"Your surroundings may change but your essence and your personality pretty much stay the same."
– Jenna Dewan

What you will learn:

- Learning about your industry's environment and the impacts of it on your company
- Recognizing how industry standards impact your work but don't have to limit it
- Finding a way to be productive, not just active, in your industry
- Standing out in a crowd to create opportunities

No matter what skills you possess, they are going to be absolutely useless without a true understanding of your environment. Let's think about the elite military personnel for a moment. Imagine that they are going to be participating in an operation in a desert-like environment. You would not expect them to show up in scuba gear, or worse yet, winter coats and snow boots, would you? No, you wouldn't. They pick everything, from their clothes to their weapons, based on the environment and what they are likely to need to be successful in that particular environment.

In the same way, you need to understand the business environment you are in and make adjustments to bring the right skills and tools to make you successful in that environment.

As anyone who has ever played a video game will understand, each level requires specific tools and abilities from your avatar. In order to get those tools or abilities, you have to conquer certain aspects of the game or overcome specific challenges. Depending on the game, you may be able to pay for those abilities or tools. Still, there is a level of effort on your part in order to be successful.

The same is true in your career. Your brand avatar is going to be the face of your own abilities, skills, and experiences. Your brand messaging will come through in all aspects, but some tailoring may be needed for each situation. However, like the characters in *Avatar*, there was a need to account for the environment. After all, as humans, they could not live in the planet's natural atmosphere. They needed specific gear to survive. I challenge you to determine what gear you need to survive in your professional environment.

You want to be able to turn that survival into thriving, but the most important thing is first to understand the environment and what is necessary to work within it. Let's start by focusing in on your company, specifically those that you are working within your department.

What Makes Your Department and Company Unique?

The environment of your department, workgroup, or company is the one you are going to function in the most often. As a result, you need to know the environment, which also means knowing how they feel about you. If you want to create change to boost your career, then you first need to understand what is normal and master it.

Too often, individuals think that blending in is a bad thing for their career, and they often end up becoming a rampaging bull through their department, regardless of whether that actually will help them to be successful. You need the knowledge of your environment to make the right choices and adjustments to your avatar. After all, you do not want to bring a water gun to a snowball fight.

Mastering your environment means understanding how the network of influence works between the members of your workgroup. When you know how to get things done in your workgroup, you can start to expand your knowledge to include your department, and even extend further into the company's hierarchy. The point is to create an understanding of the framework of your environment so that you can master it and then excel in that same environment.

Building your reputation in any environment, be it professional or personal, requires knowing how people are perceiving you in your shared environment. After all, if you don't understand that, it will be impossible to make any adjustments to bring your reputation into line with where you want to go.

Once you understand how you are viewed, and the impression that you give, you can begin to adjust it to reflect the environment better. This is the moment when you start to demonstrate a mastery of the environment that you are in. I can't tell you how many times individuals have said that they want to advance, but do not consider perceptions of themselves in the workplace.

Too often, you can have the right skills and experience, but be viewed as lazy or unmotivated. It can be hard to convince individuals to give you a chance if they believe that you are not going to take advantage of it. Instead, those opportunities end up going to others, even though you may do your job effectively. Perceptions open doors or slam them shut!

Others might see you as pushy, always trying to order others around, even though you might not have a grasp on what needs to be done or be in charge. Those who are perceived as pushy can find themselves struggling to get people to do what they ask because they are seen as overstepping and unwilling to listen to the ideas of others.

This perception is easily related to the know-it-all individual. The perception is they are unwilling to hear ideas or explore other options because they already know the best way to get things accomplished. Resentment can build against those perceived as a know-it-all, simply because those who work with them do not feel as if they are respected, or that their contribution is valued.

Another common perception that can impact how others interact with you is if you are perceived to be overly negative: the "sky is always falling, the department is in trouble, the company is closing, and we are all getting fired" type of negativity. I am sure you have run into individuals at work or in your personal life who drive you crazy because no matter how good the information is that you are given, they can find something wrong: "The sales numbers were an increase over last month." "Well, we still missed the goal, and that was only because of a couple of big orders that we won't have next month." If your company gives away coffee and donuts in the morning, these individuals complain about the quality of the coffee and that the donuts are stale. You get what I mean. It is always about finding what is wrong in a situation, instead of what is right. That kind of perception of you can make people avoid working with you, or even worse, leave you struggling to get promotions because you are perceived as hard to deal with by the leadership.

Do you see the point? All these types of perceptions can cause stumbling blocks in your ability to take gigantic leaps in your career. You need to be able to recognize how people perceive you, and then use your avatar to change that perception to one that will benefit you.

Take dating, for instance. If you want to date someone, you are going to do your best to make a good first impression. Over time, however, you might start to slip into old habits or ways of doing things, so that your current behavior alters the first impression. It can mean the end of the relationship, as they realize that you might not be the right person for them after all. Perceptions create reality, and you need to understand the perception that you are creating before you can truly start to make the changes necessary to alter the perception.

With that being said, let's shift outside of your company into the larger industry, and focus on how mastering your environment comes into play.

Knowing How You are Perceived in Your Industry

An industry environment, according to the Business Dictionary[2], is the "overall, economic, regulatory, social, and political conditions that affect all participants in an industrial market in a similar way and cannot readily be influenced by marketing. The industry environment experienced by a business can include such things as demographics, lifestyle shifts, and economic cycles."

With that in mind, I want you to take a minute to think about your perceptions of your industry. You might think of a few key individuals who demonstrate the best of your industry, and you might also easily be able to name a few individuals who do not reflect well on your industry. Now I want to ask you: Where do you fall? The reason is that no matter how hard you work, you need to understand how you are perceived, to make the right connections to impact your career positively.

---

[2] https://www.businessdictionary.com/definition/industry-environment.html

It is about mastering the environment before you can make changes in it. You too can have a huge impact on your industry's environment, but first, you have to be perceived as someone who brings relevant experience, skills, and innovation to the table. Looking for innovation starts by understanding where the industry stands right now, and its environment. Do you know the key players? Who leads and who follows? What companies are leading in developing best practices? Is your company always playing catch up?

When you work for a company that is playing catch up, it can impact how you are perceived in your industry. You could be seen as someone who can't make a difference because you aren't making one where you are.

Regulations Impact the Industry Environment

Regulatory changes can often have the biggest impact on an industry. I am sure that if you took a few minutes, you could probably list multiple areas of your business that have regulatory considerations, which must be taken into account when determining processes when making changes to specific departments, or even when considering taking on new product options or services.

"If you could get all the people in the organization rowing in the same direction, you could dominate any industry, in any market, against any competition, at any time."
– Patrick Lencioni

Many regulatory aspects of an industry can impact safety for the workers, and certain aspects must be followed for a product to be considered safe to sell or to protect consumers from the predatory aspects of that industry. Banking is often in the news for regulatory reasons. It might be that the industry is pushing back on regulations, saying that they are too much, or consumers' agencies arguing that there are not enough regulations in place on the industry.

The point is not to argue if the banking industry should be regulated or not, and to what degree they should be regulated, but to acknowledge that in order to practice in the financial realm, a company is going to face regulations.

In your industry as well, you likely have regulations on various aspects that impact how you do business. Depending on your position in the company, you may have a greater understanding of the impact of those regulations than someone that may work on the front line. I am speaking about the costs in particular. To comply with the regulations for your industry, you are likely going to need to devote manpower and other resources to compliance. Those hours and resources are not making you money, and the return on investment is simply that you get to keep doing business. It becomes part of the overhead, which can drive how your company prices its products and services, in order to cover or recoup those costs.

The regulations and the costs associated with them may mean less capital is available for growth projects, such as buying new equipment, expanding the product lines, or even hiring new employees. Now, a company may still be successful at growing, in spite of the costs associated with regulations, but there may still be limits on how much they grow in a given period.

> *"You need to turn over every rock and open every door to learn your industry. This process never ends."*
> **– Mark Cuban**

Regulations in themselves are not necessarily bad or inherently negative. Many of them were created with a specific result in mind. For example, it could be to protect the environment by limiting the number of pollutants in the air, earth, or water. Complying may be more expensive for a company, but there are also benefits to the company as well. Think about the marketing aspects for a company that can tout their environmental efforts. Now, they might not refer to the fact that they are required to do so by the regulations of the government, but they are certainly going to use it to their advantage.

When you take the time to understand the forces at work on your industry, and how they are going to impact your company or department, then you are taking the time to master your environment. Now you have a greater understanding of how one change can have a ripple effect. Compliance may not only be more expensive but may require multiple smaller changes or additional work in multiple departments.

Once your knowledge is greater in these areas, you are in the best position to stand out by bringing innovative ideas to the table. Too often, individuals want to make change without truly understanding the environment or the ripple effect that their change could have.

You do not want to be short-sighted. Have a broad and long-range vision for the impact of change, not one focused on the short-term and immediate needs of the department or industry.

Remember, when you create change, you are also going to impact how you are perceived in your industry. Think about the executive in charge of talent at the London office of Decca Records. Back in 1962, the Beatles auditioned for him. He turned them down, telling their manager that groups were out, and he didn't like their sound. Decades later, the Beatles have sold over 2 billion albums, and he is seen as the man that missed a great opportunity. A few years after that, when the Beatles were moving up the charts, I am sure his reputation in the music industry was junk.

Another great example of how perception in an industry can be altered by not understanding the environment and being innovative is the case of Kodak. The company had developed the first digital camera, in 1975, but then sat on it. Afraid it would cannibalize their film business, the company ended up waiting too long, and the technology they initially developed is now the core technology for most cell phones. At the same time, their film business has been cannibalized by a world devoted to digital innovation.

My point is that you need to be aware of the environment, understand it, and then make changes, but also be aware that when you don't make changes or make them without understanding the environment, it negatively impacts perceptions of you in your industry, which can have a long-term effect on your ability to grow your career. That understanding of the environment can help you to make suggestions that move the industry into new directions, and put you light years ahead of your competition.

"Don't underestimate the power of your vision to change the world. Whether that world is your office, your community, an industry or a global movement, you need to have a core belief that what you contribute can fundamentally change the paradigm or way of thinking about problems."
– Leroy Hood

I focused on regulations, but there are clearly other aspects of the industry environment that can play a part in influencing how your company does business.

Think about the culture of your work environment. In your department, is the environment laid back or more formal? What type of language is used? I know some companies where slang is a part of everyday life, in conversations, presentations, and even emails. Other companies frown on the use of slang.

Dress how you want to be addressed. Not every company has a dress code written down, but if you observe the individuals in your department and the leadership, you will quickly figure out which type of dress code you need to follow. For instance, if the boss comes in jeans and t-shirts, he is setting a casual culture, one that you might see others following. The boss that wears suits into the office every day, however, might frown on a casual approach to dress, even if it is not enshrined in the official handbook.

If you want to be taken seriously, then you need to show that in how you present yourself. Granted, the culture might be less formal, but to get where you want to go, you may present yourself differently, allowing your dress to help you stand out positively.

A culture can be formal or laid back, but the point is that you need to understand it, so you can move through it effectively to create your next opportunity.

Part of the culture is the work/life balance. Your company might have a culture of being friendly to workers with families, but your department head might feel differently. That means you might find yourself penalized at a departmental level for following company policy about taking time off for family events. These penalties could come in the form of not being offered key projects or being overlooked for promotions because you are not 100% *in the game.* Granted, you could go above them and complain, but it might not work in your favor. Understanding the culture can help you to make the adjustments in how you do your work to meet the demands of the department leadership, while still allowing you to take advantage of the culture of your company.

Depending on the culture, you might need to make adjustments to your brand avatar to be able to connect and get things done. It is not always easy. Workplace culture is defined by the individuals within the workplace but pushed by the leadership. If your leaders are more formal than you are going to want to present yourself more formally, even if others don't. It is about creating a perception that will benefit you and help you to stand out for the leadership.

Industries themselves also have a culture—one that can be more playful or one that demands a serious presentation. Think about the world of tech. Innovation is constant, but many of the individuals are dressed less formally and are focused more on talking with their machines and writing code. The focus is on the output, not the process. In the banking industry, however, there is a formal atmosphere that is reflected in your dress, presentations, and even how you speak. The process can be just as critical as the outcome.

I need you to recognize that understanding your environment starts at your department's culture and norms, working up to the company's culture and norms, and then finally, your industry's culture and norms. Time and again, the point is to make change, you need to have a clear understanding of how things are done, and recognize that making an impact is going to make you stand out. Perceptions of you are going to be altered, but you need to target the perceptions of those who can open doors. After all, you can bring fresh, innovative ideas to your employer, giving them the ability to turn what could be a negative into a positive. In the end, you want your workgroup and team to see you as an individual who can get the job done. You might not always be liked, but the results are key to helping you take those boosts.

Mastering your industry's environment to produce those results is often about understanding its norms and how those impact the culture.

Knowing Industry Norms

These industry norms can be very different from one industry to another. These norms are an accepted standard or way of behaving or doing things that most people agree with. I can think of hundreds of industries where a specific set of standards are used to determine if the product or services are bad, good, or the best. These standards or industry norms provide a consistent way of doing things or producing products that would be acceptable to the whole industry.

Industry standards are a set of criteria within an industry, relating to the standard functioning and carrying out of operations in their respective fields of production, as defined by U.S. Legal[3]. This type of standardization is a quality check for any industry, and can also be a crucial tool for developing, as well as meeting, the goals of a specific industry.

For instance, in manufacturing, companies can achieve various ISO levels. Doing so means that they have completed the qualifications necessary to meet those standards. It can open up additional opportunities to create growth in sales and production, as well as give them another marketing tool. However, that also means that they are going to have to maintain those very specific standards to keep that designation.

In the restaurant business, industry standards help to determine if a restaurant is going to be profitable or not. For instance, if food costs exceed the industry standard, a restaurant is likely to struggle more than one that manages their food costs more effectively. In analyzing a business, an owner often can look to industry standards to help find ways to adjust.

Another benefit that industry standards provide is consistency. As a consumer, you want consistency in the products and services you buy on a regular basis. Now, imagine if every time you picked up an Apple product, their iconic home button was in a different spot. That would get frustrating!

[3] https://definitions.uslegal.com/i/industrial-standards/

On a broader scale, the cell phone industry puts the speaker for your ear in the same general spot on every phone. You don't pick up a Samsung and find the speaker for your ear on the back, and the microphone on the front. Regardless of the phone or brand that you buy, these basic things are in the same place consistently.

When you understand your industry's norms, then you can take it to the next level and find ways to break out of those norms to create new ones. Yes, I am talking about setting the latest industry trends, instead of merely following in the treads of others. Being able to talk knowledgeably about what is standard now, and what could be possible, will help you stand out among your peers.

"You have to have a big vision and take very small steps to get there. You have to be humble as you execute but visionary and gigantic in terms of your aspiration. In the Internet industry, it's not about grand innovation, it's about a lot of little innovations: every day, every week, every month, making something a little bit better."
– Jason Calacanis

Too often, individuals use standards as a means to keep themselves from moving forward. Resistance to change can come from the phrase, "Well, that is how we do it!" Think about the individuals in your company, and even in your industry, that use that phrase, or a similar one, to resist any new idea or concept. Change is critical to keep an industry or company from stagnating.

You might feel that you are not creative enough to contribute that out-of-the-box thinking. In fact, you might have often used that "always done this way" excuse yourself from time to time. To create explosive growth in your career, you need to be willing to take those leaps of faith, and creative thinking, to change how your industry perceives you.

Many of us move throughout our industries, serving as consultants, executives, and in sales or marketing. We all learn the industry norms or standards and use them as the foundation for what we believe is possible in the industry. Best practices have been formed in many industries, taking the idea of industry norms to a new level.

"Offer someone the opportunity to rebuild a company or reinvent an industry as the primary incentive, and it will attract those drawn to the challenge first and the money second."
– Simon Sinek

Can you, someone who may be intimately familiar with those industry norms and best practices, be the one who creates the next best practice? It is possible, and that kind of initiative can make you stand out in a crowd. After all, many of the individuals that you are competing with daily have the same level of skills that you have, and likely similar knowledge and experiences. If you want to create the great leaps in your career, then you need to bring something to the table that they do not. With that in mind, let's talk about how important it is to be productive, instead of just active.

Activity versus Productivity

Depending on the industry, there are many ways to be active without being productive. While someone might be active in an industry, that does not mean they are productive. In fact, you may find that for all their activity, little is actually accomplished at the end of the day. Productivity, on the other hand, can contribute to progress and moving a task forward, even if there are limited levels of activity.

Think of a production line in a manufacturing plant. Part of what makes these lines so effective is that they limit activity through processes, thus maximizing productivity for the manufacturing plant. The point is that processes create productivity, instead of just activity that produces nothing.

To help an industry grow, it needs to be productive, not just active. The same could be said to be true of anyone looking to make leaps in their career. Do not limit yourself to industry norms or just being active in your industry. Find ways to create productivity. That might mean drawing in ideas from other industries, even if they don't appear on the surface to be related at all. Doing so will give others a different perception of you, perhaps allowing you to become a perceived expert in your field.

"I've helped some of my classmates on how to strategize to get to the next level of their businesses. And it's interesting, because here I am sitting there from the entertainment industry and the fashion industry, and I'm giving a billionaire that has a business that's been in his family for 300 years – I'm giving him advice about strategy!"
– Tyra Banks

Part of productivity is doing meaningful work, which gives value to the process or end product/service. Meaningful work provides value to your leadership, making them see you in a different light. For instance, when you do your job, are you looking for connections to others and how you could add value to the process by utilizing those connections more fully? Perhaps there is a part of the process that needs more tweaking to get the most benefit out of it. The point is that you can do your job, or you can focus on finding ways to do your job even better. You can become a value-added piece to the process, and that can help you to stand out from the crowd.

Busy work is often associated with work that you do to fill the hours but often translates to little more than pushing papers from one pile to another. It could be tasks that need to be done but might not need to take up the amount of time that they do now. It could be something that you streamline but has been viewed as a way to fill the day and avoid taking on additional tasks or projects.

Note how you can be perceived as someone who is productive, involved in adding value to the company through meaningful work, or someone who just fills the days to collect a check. These perceptions can greatly impact your ability to take leaps in your career because when you are associated with busy work, you are not seen as a valuable addition or someone who should be rewarded for their efforts with opportunities.

Productivity can also impact how you are viewed as a leader. Taking career leaps means being able to lead, and if you are perceived as sitting back and letting others take the lead, then you are not going to be seen as someone who can handle the challenges faced by your department or company. Notice that the point is not the work you actually do, but how you are perceived as you accomplish it.

When people in the industry look to you for leadership, that translates into career opportunities that you might not have anticipated. I want you to start focusing on how you can use your brand avatar, to not only explore your environment but study it with the desire to master it, and then excel within it.

Standing Out in the Crowd

When it comes to standing out in the crowd, it generally is associated with individuals taking notice of you. Merriam-Webster[4] defines it as "to be unusual in a good way," although I know individuals who stand out, but not in a good way. Think of the *black sheep* of a family, for instance.

Those in a particular industry might be known for the ruthless way that they do business, or for a demanding nature. Movies have been

[4] https://www.miriam-webster.com/dictionary/
stand%20out%20from%20the%20crowd

created around the idea of a demanding boss that everyone fears to cross, while at the same time, is secretly admired for their ability to get things done, both in their companies and within their industry. Part of standing out is the impression that you make within your company and your industry as a whole.

Here are a few ways to make sure that you are standing out, and not just blending in:

1. **Know Yourself and Your Reason Why** – Over and over again, I have talked about knowing who you are, including your values and beliefs. Still, while you might know yourself, it is important to understand how you come across to others. Take the time to get feedback from others, so that you know how you come across. Then use that information to target how you appear in a crowd accurately, but also the areas that you might need to work on. At the same time, clearly understanding your motivation helps you to keep going, and makes you easy to relate to for others.

2. **Be Conscientious and Confident** – When you are conscientious, be it about being on time, being prepared, or just honoring your commitments, it gives a powerful impression of who you are and what it can be like to work with you. Confidence is about showing that you believe in what you are trying to accomplish and that you can create what you envision. Part of that confidence is recognizing that you are not afraid of obstacles or challenges, and that will make you stand out.

3. **Cultivate Emotional Intelligence** – Part of getting ahead means being able to manage your emotions and at the same time relate to others. Let's face it, those who can display emotional intelligence attract others who are looking to connect with someone who has their act together, as well as displaying competence and capability.

4. **Be Response-able as You Lead with Excellence** – When you remember to follow through, then it is possible to stand out from those who drop the ball and don't follow up. Respond to others, and you will stand out as being respectful of others, and as accountable. It will complement the idea that you value quality. When you lead with excellence, you are prepared to deliver high-quality work, and that also helps you to stand out from those in your company.

Throughout the process of standing out, you need to remember to take yourself seriously. I forget who said this first but there is a saying, "If you are hard on yourself, the world will be easy on you but if you are easy on yourself, the world will be hard on you." Always strive for excellence in what you do. Become a master at your craft. When your employers, and those in the industry, see that you are constantly honing and developing your skills, it will draw attention to who you are and what you can bring to the table. Recognize that part of standing out means not always focusing on yourself, but instead, focusing on being interested in others, asking questions, and being a good listener. Note that in this paragraph, I have already listed a few of the important qualities that will help you to stand out from all the rest in your industry.

Wrap Up for Chapter 5 (Understanding Your Environment)

- Learn the environmental norms to understand your workgroup, company, or industry better.
- Master your environment before you attempt to change it.
- Recognize that how you are perceived in your department, company, or industry will impact your ability to create change, and can open or limit your opportunities.
- Once you know your environment, do not be afraid to stand out and innovate. Doing so gives you the chance to grow your reputation.

Now, I want to focus on *what frustrates you about everyone else*, and how you might be frustrating someone else (Remember those perceptions!), which will help you turn your frustrations into a source of energy, to help you create real momentum in your career.

Chapter 6

What Frustrates You About Everyone Else

"Expectation is the mother of all frustration."
– Antonio Banderas

What you will learn:

- To recognize that frustrations are going to happen
- Owning your power to act or react to your frustrations
- How to deal with your frustrations and make them work for you

No matter the professional environment that you find yourself in, there are going to be elements of it that do not appeal to you. Those elements could be the people that you are working with, processes that might be less than efficient, or even a boss focused more on promoting himself instead of the interests of the department or company.

These elements are a reality that you will have to adjust to and learn to deal with, even if you don't always appreciate them. Part of this is the reality that you have expectations that are not being met.

Time and again, you create expectations about how you want a situation to play out, how you want someone to react, or even how you anticipate feeling after the situation is over. Those expectations, when they are not met, often result in your feelings of frustration, anger, or stress.

"Expectation is the mother of all frustration."
– Antonio Banderas

When it comes to using your brand avatar to create the level of success you want in your career, you have to remember you determine how you are going to react to any given set of circumstances. Your avatar is controlled by you, not by those around you. With that in mind, let's identify a few of the things that you wish you could change in the people, places, and things that you are surrounded by.

What Do You Wish You Could Change in People/Places/ Things

To be honest, you and I both have a wish list of things that we wish we could change about various parts of our lives and those involved in it. That wish list might be extensive. In your professional life, in particular, you might have a long list of those items. Here are just a few that come to mind:

- **Lack of Leadership** – Your department head or workgroup manager might be good at paying attention to details, but they might not be good at delegating or leading the team during busy times or transitions in the company. It may lead to frustration, especially when you feel that a lack of direction is complicating your job, or that multiple individuals are doing the same task different ways, leading to multiple processes.

- **Lack of Consistent Processes** – When there are no consistent processes, it becomes the Wild West in terms of how things are accomplished. Therefore, you find frustration building, and morale lowering, simply because no one knows how to get something done without feeling as if they are starting from scratch every single time.

- **Lack of Recognition** – There is always going to be a worker that does the most (or thinks that they do the most). If their efforts are not acknowledged by their co-workers or the bosses, then it can be frustrating. Perhaps you have experienced a lack of appreciation in the past. When it happens, you feel less motivated to keep working at the same level, and your loyalty, quality, and work ethic can start to suffer.

- **Inconsistent Workloads** – It can often be said that those who are consistent and conscientious become the ones that end up doing a majority of the work. This reality occurs because those who do not follow through get shifted off onto other projects, and the workload shifts to those that the boss feels confident will get the work done. However, after a while, that increasing workload can get overwhelming and lead to increasing frustration with your professional environment.

- **Personal Conflicts** – You may find that you have personal conflicts with those in your workgroup, which bleeds over into how you work together. Over time, it can make you feel frustrated every time you deal with that individual, making it difficult for you to listen to them or work effectively with them.

- **Organizational Challenges** – Your company might be changing, and those changes may not be communicated effectively throughout the company. The result could be a high level of frustration, as individuals are unclear of their role in the company, or whether they may be leaving the company altogether.

As you can see, there are multiple areas in which you might find yourself frustrated or overwhelmed in your career. How can you tackle these issues effectively and use them to move you forward in your career?

"Success is not built on success. It's built on failure. It's built on frustration. Sometimes it's built on catastrophe."
– Sumner Redstone

What Have You Done/Not Done to Solve Those Frustrations

I want to bring you back to your expectations as part of the discussion about what you can do to address your frustrations. The reason I want to focus on your expectations is because you can control your expectations. You cannot control people or the circumstances that you are presented with daily.

First, I want you to look at a situation that is frustrating you, and ask yourself, "What are my expectations that are not being met?" Often, it starts by accessing those expectations and asking yourself if you have set them too high, or if you have not taken into account additional aspects of the situation that are now having a bearing on the situation.

"I was an accomplice in my own frustration."
– Peter Shaffer

Imagine that your frustration comes from a lack of leadership. You might have just been assigned to a new boss and are looking for direction from that individual, but it might not be materializing. Perhaps you need to evaluate the situation from their perspective. Could they be expecting you to already have a working knowledge of their department's procedures and processes? Have you taken the time to express a need for additional training? Often times, you need to be willing to ask for what you need, instead of waiting for it to come to you.

Expectations also work in reverse. Perhaps you are setting your expectations for yourself too low, not pushing yourself to reach further or stand out in the crowd. When you are honest with yourself, you can access what you are doing that could be contributing to your frustration level. It could be that you are being resistant to the leadership being given, instead of accepting their role in your department.

The point is that you have the power to act, instead of just complaining about it or stewing in your frustration. Time and again, you are going to find that those who spend time complaining or acting out negatively based on their frustration, are not necessarily making a good impression on the leaders that could open up opportunities to them.

When you feel a lack of appreciation, for example, you might consider talking with your boss about areas that you could improve in to achieve recognition. Your efforts can keep you motivated, while showing your boss that you are focused on giving your best. Often, simply making an effort to connect with your boss can allow them to give you that recognition and appreciation that you need.

Also, be willing to show appreciation for the efforts of others. You might be surprised at how quickly they return the favor. You also create a level of goodwill with your co-workers, one that can benefit you down the line as you are trying to influence them in a leadership position. When you take the time to acknowledge others and their efforts, it begins a process that spreads goodwill throughout your department. After all, if you want to be recognized for the work you do, then it should be easy to see why others will want the same.

Frustration levels are not always easy to control. You may find yourself reacting before taking the time to consciously determine your response. It can be a process to stop before you move down an emotional track uncontrolled. Your avatar is a personification of your brand and the message that you want to transmit professionally. I would argue that you can use that avatar to help you successfully address your frustration.

"It is hardly possible to build anything if frustration, bitterness, and a mood of helplessness prevail."
– Lech Walesa

Another way to address frustration is to give yourself an outlet. You may not be able to make changes in your department or company, but you can provide yourself the means to bring your frustration level down. Some individuals choose exercise, journaling, or even meditation as their outlet.

All of these can provide you with the ability to take your mind off your frustration, clear your head, and then give yourself a way to move forward. Perhaps an idea to address the issue causing frustration will come forward, but even if it doesn't, you are providing your body and mind with an outlet to get rid of the aggression and negative energy created by the feeling of frustration.

Often, when you are frustrated, you are acting out of emotion and not out of your conscious mindset. Negative energy is building up, and that can impact your ability to do your best work or effectively communicate with others. Finding ways to release that negative energy in a constructive way can serve you well, because it can help you to keep those emotions in check, allowing you to present your best self professionally.

"If you so choose, every mistake can lead to greater understanding and effectiveness. If you so choose, every frustration can help you to be more patient and more persistent."
– Ralph Marston

Take a moment and recognize that you can also learn from your frustration. Instead of allowing it to block you from seeing potential opportunities, use it to help you create them. Are you are frustrated because of a lack of processes? Then set about creating them. Document the best way that you have found to complete the task, and present it to your boss or manager. You are taking the initiative to address your frustration. In the process, you might also be addressing a frustration that others have.

The point is to use your frustration as momentum to create real change in your professional life. That *thinking outside of the box* also gives you the opportunity to showcase your abilities, and can bring you to the attention of the leadership in your company or industry. If you want to take big leaps in your career, it is important to use your avatar to get yourself noticed for solving problems, instead of just complaining about what is not working.

> **"Needing to have things perfect is the surest way
> to immobilize yourself with frustration."**
> **– Wayne Dyer**

Over and over again, I find that those individuals who achieve the most, use their frustrations to their advantage. They see the opportunities that are presented in addressing that frustration, then take advantage of those opportunities. Granted, frustrations related to your interactions with co-workers and team members might not be so easy to solve. It may be a case of choosing how you will respond to them, and then making the conscious choice not to respond in a negative way.

When you choose a different response, you may find that it genders a different response from others. Control what you can, and then let go of what you can't. Plus, if you allow that frustration with an individual to build, it can begin to block your ability to accomplish what you want to achieve in your position. After all, every position that you are in is actually a stepping stone to where you want to go next.

Consider trying to find the good in that individual, and then make a point to acknowledge them for it. You may just think it is a small thing, but focusing on the positive of an individual, and recognizing them for it, can be key to easing tensions and building a better relationship, which can positively impact the whole department.

Do not be quick to assume that you can gain nothing by learning to work with those that are frustrating or can present challenges to getting something done. Often, it can be a way to practice a different set of leadership skills. The reality is that to get things done in your career, you are going to need to find a way to work with all kinds of personalities, viewpoints, and skill sets.

I talk frequently about perception, and I find that it plays a lot into how I interact with others. If I alter my perception of others, then I also find myself interacting with them differently. Think of a tapestry. If you look at the back of it, there is clearly a big mess of strings and knots that are holding the tapestry together. Now, turn it over to the front, and you can see what a beautiful piece it is. Your perceptions of others often depend on what side of them you see. Recognize, however, that there is more to an individual than just that side you see.

Changing How You Perceive Others

The way that you perceive others is the way that they are likely to be, in large part because, subconsciously, we all perform according to perceived expectations. In order to improve a relationship, you need to evolve your perception of that individual to how you want to perceive them, and the expectations that you want to have for them. Simply put, if you change how you see an individual, then you are going to change how you relate to them and how you perceive them. When you respond to individuals with praise and positive emotions, then you are essentially changing them by changing your perceptions.

Creating this change can start by painting a positive picture in your head of your co-worker or teammate. Take notice of all the good things the individual does. See their strengths and qualities they bring to the table. Notice I am talking about changing your focus from the negative to the positive.

Your perceptions of the world itself might also need to be overhauled. If you want to be successful in your career, you need to see difficult circumstances, or even failures, as part of the learning curve. Focus on overcoming the challenge, instead of seeing it as an obstacle stopping you dead in your tracks. Be aware that much of your success and how far you go in your career is based on how you perceive various circumstances and individuals that you encounter throughout your career.

If you are not receiving the opportunities you want or achieving your goals, perhaps you need to re-evaluate your perceptions. Could you be limiting yourself?

The source of your perceptions is likely rooted in how you grew up, the influences you were exposed to, and then your own experiences over time. Those sources become an automatic subconscious filter, one that you don't even realize is influencing your perceptions. I find it critical to stop from time to time and consciously access why I have the perception that I have, and if it needs to be altered.

Your brain creates filters that help to build your perceptions of individuals and situations. It is important to recognize that you can change those filters. Once you do, your perceptions can change. If you change your perceptions, you will find that others respond differently to you.

Marriage is a great example of this point. When you perceive that your marriage mate does not care, then you are going to act accordingly. However, when you change that perception, you start to see their behavior in a new light and respond accordingly.

Your boss and co-workers are part of your professional life. You could change directions in the relationship by changing your perceptions.

Recognize that while not everyone will immediately turn into sunshine and roses, you will be able to respond differently, and impact your reputation in your company.

I find it is easy to get sucked into a negative path of thinking, but once you are on that path, you can quickly find that you are creating barriers in your mind, blocking you from achieving your goals. Frustration can easily suck you into negative thinking. Instead of allowing that, look at your frustration as inspiration to address the issue and grow from your experiences. Leaders are ones who can take a negative experience and turn it into a beneficial teaching moment for themselves and possibly others.

Granted, you may feel that your perceptions are accurate and valid. Challenging those perceptions from time to time, however, are key to keeping you moving forward and not getting bogged down in your frustrations with individuals or circumstances. I want you to recognize that your perceptions could also be blocking your creativity and the special abilities that make you valuable and unique in your professional career.

Wrap Up for Chapter 6 (What Frustrates You About Everyone Else)

- Recognize that you will deal with frustrating individuals, situations, and leadership.
- Focus on changing your perceptions to create change in others.
- Use frustrations as motivation to come up with solutions, thus creating professional opportunities for yourself.

As you can see, frustrations do not have to derail your career or leave you unable to enjoy what you do for a living. Instead, they can be the motivation to help you move forward. Your unique ability to turn a frustration into a positive can end up giving you a leg up, and help you to stand out.

With that in mind, in the next chapter, let's focus on *What Makes You So Damn Special.* I want to focus on defining whether you are a lemming, a rebel, or a leader, which will help you magnify your strengths, and how you can give those strengths to your avatar.

Chapter 7

What Makes You So Damn Special?

**"Don't ever doubt yourselves
or waste a second of your life.
It's too short, and you're too special."
– Ariana Grande**

What you will learn:

- How to use being a lemming to your advantage
- The benefits of being a rebel
- Why being a leader is critical to your career

In previous chapters, I focused on what you wanted out of your career, how to build a brand avatar to use to achieve these goals, and how you need to understand your environment in order to create the perceptions you need to be successful. Now that you have put in the work to blend in, I want to turn the corner and help you to stand out.

Why is it so important to stand out? Let's face it, the person who shows up to work and consciously does their job, without making a splash, is unlikely to move up in their career. The ones that show up to work, and do their job with a focus on how to do it better—with a focus on creating innovative solutions for their clients or bosses—those are the individuals making strides in their careers, and are not afraid to let the world know what they are doing.

I am not saying that those individuals doing their jobs and keeping their heads down are not coming up with innovative ideas or processes. The point is that they are not getting the credit for them, which translates into no movement.

> *"To be a great champion, you must believe you are the best.*
> *If you're not, pretend you are."*
> **– Muhammad Ali**

What makes you special is your ability to adapt your brand avatar to what is needed, based on the environment and the conditions at hand. You have the power to define those moments when you stand out from the crowd and get the credit that you deserve, and those moments when you are just barely noticeable, avoiding the potential fallout.

Have you gone to a concert or other large event? When you scan the crowd, does someone stand out to you? What made them stand out? I am sure you can describe how they were dressed, how they were acting, or the group they were with that made them stick out in your mind. That is my point! I want you to stand out in the crowd. Be that individual your boss remembers—that the president of the company looks to for ideas—and the industry expert!

When someone scans the proverbial crowd, I want them to remember you! Their perceptions are going to open doors for you or slam them shut. Being pigeon-holed into a specific slot can be the death knell to your career, especially if you do not take the time to learn how to adjust the face of your brand avatar effectively.

Let's take a trip down memory lane, back to high school, for a minute. The star quarterback is standing out in a crowd. The school is winning, and everyone loves him. Yet he is also being pigeonholed as a jock, with all the perceptions of not being able to handle schoolwork, or that his grades are the result of getting others to do the work for him.

Now, he might be a science-geek, doing amazing things with his experiments, and getting grades that put scholarships into his reach. Yet that is not the perception many have of him, and likely, that won't change. Still, he could do little to draw attention to his academic accomplishments because he wants to avoid being perceived as uncool or a dork. Perception plays into many of the decisions that you are going to make in your career, so it is important that you act in a way that produces the right perception for the current and future stages of your career.

I want you to have the perception of being an all-star while having the skills, experience, and knowledge to back it up. That is the package that will take you far in your career, and will help you to achieve your goals, objectives, and dreams.

> *"Things do not happen. Things are made to happen."*
> **– John F. Kennedy**

So, what are you? What makes you so special and unique, that you can capitalize on and make it work to take you to the next level? You are the key to creating the change you want in your career, so it is important to stand in your power.

Making progress in your career is not only about setting goals, but letting others know about those goals. Your boss should be aware of your goals, and if possible, even your boss' boss. Along with that, focus on making your bosses look good as far up the chain as possible. They will see that effort, and it can be key to opening doors that allow you to achieve your goals.

Connect with Your Boss to Stand Out

- Find ways to make your boss look good in how you perform your job daily.
- Provide support for your boss, and be someone they can count on

to go to the next level.
- Look for opportunities to support your boss in supporting their own boss.

If you don't have career goals, then it is important to set them. Without that map, years can go by without you moving forward and achieving your dreams, both personally and professionally. Do the following:

- Ask yourself what you want to be doing professionally, 1, 5, and 10 years from now.
- Define the steps necessary to reach those points.
- Vocalize those goals to others that can hold you accountable.
- Once you achieve a goal, set down and define where you want to go next.

In the next few pages, I am going to focus on three different types of individuals: the lemming, the rebel, and the leader. As you read, look at what makes each one unique, whether they stand out positively or negatively, and how you use this knowledge to your advantage as you shape your brand avatar.

Are You a Lemming?

According to Merriam-Webster[5], a lemming, in the financial sense, is "an investor who does whatever the crowd does." Granted, when it comes to your career, the idea of following the crowd blindly has a negative connection. After all, when you follow the crowd blindly, you give up your free will to a large degree. The crowd does not have your best interests at heart. They are not worried about your career or helping you to be successful.

---

[5] https://www.miriam-webster.com/dictionary/lemming

"You can't build a reputation on what you are going to do."
– Henry Ford

If you tend just to follow the crowd, because you do not want to make waves, then it can be hard for others to see what you can offer to their business. Giving you the chance to advance can be limited because you don't seem able to stand up for your idea, or to showcase your skills. Thinking for yourself and being able to innovate, as well as critical thinking, are key to not being labeled a lemming.

When it comes to following the crowd, you run the risk of following them right to catastrophe, instead of recognizing how to avoid that catastrophe. For instance, a leader might be focused on doing things a certain way, even though it slows down production or could risk the department's ability to meet its goals. Following that leader's course of action could spell disaster for those who follow that lead, instead of trying to stand out within the company beyond your department.

After all, when change is coming, people can burrow down and be unwilling to open their mind. If you are a lemming, you could follow the crowd as they engage in that behavior. Don't be a lemming. Open your mind to change, and embrace the possibilities.

"I'd rather attempt to do something great, and fail,
than attempt to do nothing and succeed."
– Robert Schuller

Being a lemming, however, can have its advantages. When you go with the crowd, you can get the lay of the land or a better understanding of the environment. A lemming's actions can help you to learn what is expected and what is frowned upon. Your brand avatar can be a lemming for a period of time, allowing you to figure out who are the influencers and who are the individuals who would make good connections for you as you move forward.

During this time, use your lemming status to help you plan your next move that will allow you to stand out. Being a lemming can be strategic, but once you decide it is time to stand out for your boss, then the knowledge you gained as a lemming can be put to good use.

For instance, in your lemming status, you may have observed a few trouble spots in a process that is negatively impacting sales or productivity. When you stand out, it could be by sharing with your boss a solution to those trouble spots. Now you are making them look good by solving the issue, and standing out in their mind in the process.

That does not mean that you are going to always be a lemming, but remember, the point of a brand avatar is to be what you need to be for a given situation or environment. You are always in the position to make adjustments as the environment or culture changes. It is about putting your best foot forward, based on what is in line with your goals and objectives.

At times, you might find that you need to step outside of the lemming role, and turn into a rebel. What does that mean, and how can it be effective in moving you forward?

Are You a Rebel?

The association with the word, *rebel*, implies going against the norm, defying expectations, and perhaps even going your own way in the face of cultural and social rules. Rebels are often seen as a negative, ones that stand out, but for all the wrong reasons. Yet there are many individuals who take a rebel on for their brand avatar, and are able to benefit from it.

Remember, the point is to use these attributes to benefit you. Your brand avatar is going to adjust to the environment. Could the company you are in use a rebel? Do they need to be shaken up to get to the next level? If you are that rebel, will it benefit you in the long run, as a change maker?

> *"Motivation alone is not enough. If you have an idiot and you motivate him, now you have a motivated idiot."*
> **– Jim Rohn**

I want you to recognize that being a rebel is often about the strategy that you employ to create the ladder to the next level of your career. While there is a time and a place to be a lemming, there is also a time and place to be a rebel. It can help you to stand out to the leadership, allowing them to see you in a new light.

However, don't rebel just to say you did it. As teenagers, you and I rebelled to get attention, or just to have a crazy story to tell our kids. In business and your career, rebelling with no strategy can bring potential backlash, with negative consequences. You can end up branding yourself as a troublemaker in the industry, which is what you don't want.

The best form of being a rebel is one where you take on the established way of doing things, and promote real and constructive change. That upheaval can get you a reputation for bringing energy and *shaking things up*. Your industry reputation can grow as a result.

Every situation is going to call for something different. Being a rebel is great, but you also have to factor in the leaders of your department and company. Perhaps they do not reward that type of outside-the-box thinking. Therefore, you might find that tempering your rebel with a bit of lemming from time to time can help you to get where you need to go.

Additionally, these are attributes of your brand avatar that you can put on and take off, depending on the situation. When you use these attributes, you are using them to show off your skills, knowledge, and experience. Therefore, you need to be in strategy mode, as you determine the best one to put forward in a given situation.

"Do not let what you cannot do interfere with what you can do."
– John Wooden

The point is that a rebel is going to defy expectations. Here is another way to make the rebel work in your favor. Let's say your boss believes you are only capable of handling smaller, less detail-oriented projects. He or she has now set an expectation for you. Rebelling against that expectation means taking on more detailed work as it presents itself, thus showcasing your capabilities in a way that can lead to bigger, more detailed projects.

The point is that you are trying to change an expectation and perception, simply by rebelling against them and breaking through those expectations. It is not easy to rebel all the time, and there can be consequences that you might not expect. Still, I encourage you to look for ways that you can use this attribute to highlight what you know how to do. It gives you the potential to open new doors in your career.

Still, neither of these attributes will benefit you if you are not able to truly lead when the situation calls for it. How can leadership qualities work for you and your brand avatar?

Are You a Leader?

Everyone has moments where they can choose to lead or they can choose to follow. In that moment of choice, you can change the trajectory of your whole career. Why do I say that? Because leaders create the vision that followers implement.

Let me be clear. Being a leader has nothing to do with your title or position in the company. It doesn't happen when you reach a certain pay grade or achieve a particular promotion. I have talked about leaders in your company, primarily referring to those senior executives who set policy and procedures. Leaders are not necessarily those with a lot of charisma or good management skills. While all of these things might play into your role as a leader, the truth is that you can be a leader long before it is reflected in your title or paycheck. You can create a following and become a force to be reckoned with within your department, company, or industry.

Leadership is often a process of social influence, which maximizes the efforts of others towards the achievement of a goal, according to Kevin Kruse, author of the book, *Employee Engagement 2.0*[6]. His point was that leadership involves multiple aspects and is not limited to just having followers or people who do what you say. Leadership is not limited to your ability to influence or empower others but combines a host of qualities.

There are many paths to create effective leaders. They don't come in cookie cutter shapes and sizes but can include many styles and paths. Here are a few common elements that come into play with quality leadership.

Vision – Your vision is about making a goal real enough that you can inspire others with the possibility of what can be, instead of what is right now. Without a vision, it can be hard to lead others, because they will not have something to buy into.

Motivation – Any good leader finds a way to motivate their people. They are channeling the energy and professional potential of their coworkers to achieve objectives. No sports movie would be

[6] https://www.forbes.com/sites/kevinkruse/2013/04/09/what-is-leadership/#46351b915b90

complete without the motivational speech by a coach who fires up the team right before they go on to win the big game. The point is that motivation fires people up and gets them excited to achieve.

Support – Leaders are supportive of their people. This means providing them the tools they need, the training they need, and recognition of their efforts. Teachers in the public-school system often find themselves without the tools they need, or time for training, and a lack of recognition for their efforts. As a result, the industry suffers from a morale problem. My point is that if you want to lead, then you need to recognize the importance of supporting your people.

Set the bar – Defining your expectations is critical to being a successful leader. People want to know what you expect. Without that clear definition, it can be very frustrating. While you may set the bar high, you don't want to do so and not provide support. You also need to give individuals the ability to be creative in their own right. It is okay to not have all the answers as a leader, but you need to provide the atmosphere for others to step up and give you the benefit of their skills and experiences.

Listen, then guide – Leaders are effective when they are able to listen, hear the needs of their team, and then guide them to the goal by addressing those needs. It is often true that your team has the ability, but they need you to provide the roadmap to the goal. Listening is a skill that can be developed. Make sure that you are listening to truly hear, instead of listening to respond. Take your time to respond after your team members speak, to give you time to digest what they had to say.

Take risks – Your team needs to see you take risks, so that they see it is okay to be creative and innovative. You are going to show them how to find opportunities, and that you are willing to risk failure to achieve. It also allows you to showcase that failure does not have to be a defining obstacle that stops you from moving forward, but can be a source of motivation.

Team building – People management is often one of the most difficult challenges that leaders face. Still, building a team takes effort. It involves taking responsibility for what goes wrong, and taking steps to fix it, as well as rewarding the group after a job well done or a goal achieved.

Continuous improvement – Good leaders are focused on constantly improving, and they encourage this in their team. Modeling that behavior allows you to turn individuals on your team into stars, and encourages others to make efforts to improve and grow. Your influence grows as a result.

As you can see, showcasing the attributes of a leader can give you another weapon in the arsenal of your avatar. Once you embrace the qualities of a leader, you can find opportunities to demonstrate your capabilities. Leaders are influencers, and when you can influence your team, then your career can go to the next level based on your results.

Wrap Up for Chapter 7 (What Makes You So Damn Special)

- You can be a lemming, a rebel, or a leader, based on the situation.
- Recognize that each attribute showcases your skills, experience, and abilities.
- Being a leader involves more than telling individuals what to do.
- Develop the skills of a leader, and use them even if you don't have the title.

As you can see, what makes you special is really more about skills and attributes you bring to a given situation. Often, you may highlight leadership qualities, but other situations may call for the lemming or rebel. Recognize that there are positives and negatives to the lemming and rebel, so using them as part of your long-term strategy can be key to your success.

Now, I want to focus on *constructing a transformational you*, which will help you to develop your online presence, create your network alliances, and evaluate the success of your avatar in your career.

Part 3

Become Your Brand Avatar and Start Winning

Chapter 8

Constructing a Transformational You

"Yes, your transformation will be hard. Yes, you will feel
frightened, messed up and knocked down.
Yes, you'll want to stop.
Yes, it's the best work you'll ever do."
– Robin Sharma

What you will learn:

* How to use your online presence to achieve your goals
* The importance of building alliances
* The benefits of coaching and mentoring for yourself and others
* Why you should evaluate your success

During the last few chapters, I have been focused on giving you the tools you need, to create the brand avatar that you need in order to be successful and support your path to achieving your goals. That being said, once your brand avatar is in place, you are going to need to build your network to get the best results from your avatar.

The point of all the work is to produce a brand avatar that can positively impact your present, to create the future that you have always wanted. It is not easy to step back and recognize that your hard work alone is not going to take you to the next level. Your brand avatar is going to allow you to match the perceptions of individuals with your skills, experience, and knowledge, to take your career into a new trajectory.

Part of that effort involves building relationships, especially those with others in key positions within your department, company, or industry. Once you have those relationships, you are in a position to capitalize on them with how you perform various tasks and handle specific projects. Those relationships are best described as alliances, because an alliance allows you to join forces for a common cause and a specific period of time.

In the next few pages, I want to focus on creating alliances, the importance of your online presence, the importance of coaches and mentors, and how to evaluate your success. The point of this chapter is to take what you have learned and put it into practice in a meaningful way, which will impact the trajectory of your professional life. Let's get started!

Your Online Presence

Your brand avatar should be the face of your online presence. After all, you want to keep your focus on the message and how your brand avatar is part of reaching your goals. If you become distracted from that purpose online, then you could negatively impact the progress you are making at your job in your department, company, and industry.

What do I mean by that? There are plenty of ways to get yourself noticed on social media. From Facebook to Instagram and Twitter, your thoughts, experiences, and relationships can be public. Therefore, it is always important to pause before you post. Take a couple of seconds to evaluate what you want to say, and its potential impact. You can stand for something, such as a cause or political stance, but remember that there can be backlash for that.

In the movie Avatar, changing his belief system and standing up for that change put him in direct conflict with his superiors. Your beliefs, and a desire to make them known, could also put you in direct conflict with your bosses. Recognize that there is a line between the personal and professional. While you might have a specific belief or thoughts on the president and his actions, or the latest moves in the wars of your local leaders, it might be best to leave that at home, and minimize the presence of that in your online interactions where your bosses could see them.

You are a reflection of your company and your bosses, even when you are not at work. People associate you with them, so your online presence needs to reflect that reality.

Another aspect of your online presence is in your email communication. Over and over again, you type messages and hit send, giving information to other individuals in your work group, other departments, and potentially clients. In these communications, you need to be aware of how you are presenting yourself. Again, it goes back to perceptions.

We have all written at least one snippy or sarcastic email, only to delete the draft and start again. You recognize that there is a larger impact that could be felt from sending that original email. So you temper it to convey your thoughts and information in a more constructive way. It is not always easy, especially if that individual has a habit of frustrating you. Instead of allowing that frustration to influence your online presence, you have the power to control your response to the situation and the individual, putting that frustration to work for you and not against you.

Every interaction you have online, or through an online medium, has the ability to add to the perception you want people to have of you, or to detract from it. Remember, you are trying to move forward in your career, and that involves not just making yourself look good, but being a positive reflection on your brand avatar.

With that in mind, it is important to not post political or religious opinions, or jokes that pass the PG rating. For example, Roseanne is an American comedian who made what was deemed to be a racist tweet. Once it was posted, she had backlash, which included the loss of her television show, and ended up costing many people their jobs. Production, stage hands, other actors, and all the people behind the scenes, who marketed the show and sold ads based on it, lost out. The lesson is that you need to recognize that while you might have the freedom to say and do what you want, it might not always be advantageous.

When you post those types of jokes or comments, whether you meant it to be sarcastic or not, you have essentially put yourself in the position of having to defend it, and that puts you behind the eight ball. The moral of the story is to think before you post!

At the same time, your online presence allows you to reach out to others in your company or industry to make connections. You can connect through webinars or other events, allowing you to share information regarding best practices, or connect regarding potential opportunities. I like to think of these connections as a way to brainstorm and learn from those in your industry. At the same time, you are now connecting with experts, or perhaps mentoring someone else, thus becoming an expert or authority yourself.

What I want you to do is build a network. While you might be accustomed to doing so online (Think of all your social media contacts!), I want you to focus on how you can use those same skills when it comes to building your professional career.

Building Network Alliances

Why are alliances so critical? First, they give you a stronger voice. If you are part of a network or alliance that is vocalizing for change in your company and industry, then you are more likely to be heard and your issues addressed. Unions were a huge part of the industrial revolution, simply because they provide that stronger voice for workers' rights. Today, your network might not be pursuing workers' rights, but could be pursuing a better process or other critical policy changes that could positively impact the workflow or sales.

> *"The company you keep determines how others view you.*
> *Identify with mediocrity and you will be labeled subpar.*
> *Collaborate with questionable people and your reputation*
> *becomes suspect. Guilt by association can end a career, hurt your*
> *business, and cost you friends. Choose alliances wisely or*
> *you may be condemned for someone else's sins."*
> **– Carlos Wallace, author of *Life is Not Complicated – You Are:***
> ***Turning Your Biggest Disappointments into Your Greatest Blessings***

Look at the individuals in your professional life as part of a puzzle. While that piece might not fit right now, you don't throw it away. Eventually, you find a place for every piece to create a beautiful puzzle. Your professional network is much the same way. Just because you might not see where some individual fits right now, does not mean that they might not have a place later on. Do not be quick to dismiss connections, because they could be potential opportunities.

Your alliances do not always have to be formal ones. They can be informal, short-term, and even be focused on one particular issue or point. You might find that you strategize the best way to address a challenge in your company, but later, that alliance dissolves as you move on to the next challenge or issue. Remember, alliances are not permanent but have flexibility.

There are several practical steps to building any alliance, as listed below:

- **Start Right Away** – Building an alliance should be part of your career action plan, and the sooner you start, the sooner you can benefit from your alliance.
- **Keep it Small** – When you are trying to build an alliance, it might be easy to reach out to a large number of individuals, but that might backfire, as the group loses focus. Therefore, it is important to start small and then build your alliance organically. While you may have a specific strategy in mind initially, the needs of your alliance may alter that strategy over time.
- **Why Do You Need an Alliance?** – It can be easy to focus on building an alliance, but you need to know why an alliance with one particular individual or group is critical versus another. Your why might be to exchange information or might be focused on creating a larger impact in your department, based on specific activities. The point is to determine why you need the alliance, and then build it around that goal. The more collaboration that you need, the more complicated your alliance can become.
- **Find the Key Stakeholders** – When you are invested in something, then you work hard to achieve the best outcome. You have skin in the game. When you want to build an alliance, you need to find individuals who also have skin in the game and are focused on the goal. Once you find those individuals, you can hold each other accountable and make true progress to achieving your desired outcome.

The main point of these alliances is dependent on what you want to achieve and how formal you want to make them. You may also find that alliances can help you to tap skills and knowledge that you do not have, allowing you to reach a goal sooner than you thought possible. Recognize that not every member of the alliance is going to have the same goals so that they will ebb and flow accordingly.

"Today's partners can be your competitors tomorrow. And today's competitors can be your partners tomorrow."
– Suzy Kassem, author of *Rise Up and Salute the Sun:*
The Writings of Suzy Kassem

No matter what type of alliance you create, recognize that you need to be a trustworthy partner. What I mean is that you need to follow through on your commitments, and be consistent. Even if you end up altering or ending an alliance, you still have a connection that you may be able to tap later. The point is that you want to be respectful of others, even if you don't agree with them. It reflects well on you, both now and into the future.

At the same time, you may have already created some alliances. Do not be quick to dismiss them. You may find that you need to continue to cultivate that alliance because it can have long-term benefits. I talked about making your boss, and even their boss, look good if you can. Doing so helps you to build and cultivate an alliance that can positively impact your career in many ways. Not only can it mean immediate promotions, but they also have connections and may be able to open doors for further opportunities.

That being said, I need to put in a word of caution. It can be easy to build alliances, but they are not always going to reflect well on you. As I have repeatedly mentioned, others' perceptions can impact how far you go in a department, company, or industry. Be critical in analyzing who you ally yourself with and be honest about how they are perceived. Could how they are perceived be limiting you by association?

Don't be afraid to let alliances fade, or to make changes if you see a negative impact. Remember the point of all this work is to create the career that you want to fulfill your dreams. You can inspire someone else to achieve if you are not willing to accept mediocre from anyone, not even yourself.

The Coaching and Player Concept

Have you ever played organized sports? The concept is that teams are built based on the players having different skill sets. The coach's job is to work with his team to address any weaknesses in the players by using the strengths of the other players. He can help you to identify your strengths and weaknesses, then maximize the benefits of one and mitigate the negatives of the other. A coach does not have to be successful in that field to help you be successful. All of this effort is meant to help the team work together to win games, and the individuals on the team to be successful.

Football players have to listen to their coaches and follow strict regiments to keep themselves in the best shape possible. It might include specific training camps, exercises, and even changes to their diet. Following a coach is not always easy, especially after doing things one way for years. Their knowledge can be just what that player needs to take them to the next level.

That is why it is so important to have a career coach. They are going to be able to help you to be successful in achieving your goals. Here are a few key benefits from having a coach:

- Gain knowledge and skills
- Professional socialization
- Personal support to facilitate success

You might find that your career is plateauing, and you want to jump start it. Working with a coach, you can identify weaknesses and strategies to address them. A coach will hold you accountable for not following through. Too often, you can identify the weakness, but you don't hold yourself accountable to act in a way to address it. Instead, you find yourself procrastinating. That procrastination can negatively impact your career and keep you from finding and taking advantage of critical opportunities.

Look at your career as a series of practices where you are preparing for the big game. Working with a coach means that you are sharpening your skills in such a way that you will be ready for that big opportunity when it presents itself.

Benefits of coaching include:

- Improvement of your performance, targets, and goals
- Increased openness to learning and development
- Greater ownership and responsibility
- Greater clarity of your role and objectives
- Improvement of specific skills or behavior
- Opportunity to make corrections as needed

While you might have a coach to address a specific weakness, a mentor can offer you another way to grow, by helping you to follow the path they have already walked.

Mentors can be a great way to learn because they bring a different viewpoint, a different set of skills, and a different point of view. They have been where you want to go. You need to be able to tap these sources, both for inspiration but also practical information and knowledge. It is about putting yourself on a path to grow.

I believe strongly in the benefits of mentoring. It is a critical part of your ability to grow in any industry. Depending on your company, you may find that mentors are part of their company's strategy to grow the knowledge and skills of individuals within their workforce. If your company does not offer mentorships, then seek them out for yourself. I continue to mentor individuals in a variety of professional areas, giving them a sounding board, as well as someone to hold them accountable for their actions or their lack of action. A mentor can call you out when they see you making an excuse, or not using your avatar to your benefit. If you are sabotaging yourself, they are going to point it out to you.

The fact is that a mentor looks at your situation, and where you want to go, with a clearer vision than you will. They don't have the baggage and emotional connection to the situation that you do. When you listen to them with an open mind, instead of a fixed mindset, you give yourself a chance to learn and grow, both personally and professionally.

Benefits of a mentor include:

- **Increasing Your Motivation** – Everyone in the process benefits from increased motivation. You gain a beneficial perspective, and your mentor gets a feeling of accomplishment from helping someone else. I also find that it motivates people to recognize their potential and then work to achieve, based on that potential.

- **Develop Communication Skills** – Mentoring helps you to develop better communication skills by forcing you to develop questioning and listening skills, allowing you to get better at interpreting your environment and what makes individuals in your workgroup or department and your bosses tick. Once you understand them better, you can use your avatar to deliver it.

- **Obtain New Insight** – These new perspectives and insight come from those with more experience than you have and taking advantage of that can give you a competitive edge over those in your industry and your company.

- **Flexibility** – When you work with a mentor, you can determine the learning objectives, which allows you to have more control over the process. With objectives, you and your mentor have a clear idea of what you want to achieve, particularly in relation to your career.

- **New Ideas** – Let's face it. Once you work with a mentor, you will find a sounding board and a way to tap into new ideas. Often, it is through discussions with others that inspiration comes, giving you the fresh perspective you need to solve the challenge you have been dealing with. Clearly, you can integrate their perspective, allowing you to think of the challenge in a different way that positively impacts your ability to address it successfully. You are also going to be challenged to utilize your talent and expertise to help others.

Notice that all of these aspects can be achieved by growing your alliances, including those with mentors. Do not be afraid to have several mentors. You might have a different mentor to address different aspects of your professional life. In the end, the point is that once you have a mentor, be willing to mentor others. It is a way to pay it forward and will also help you grow as you teach and learn with others.

I continue to have mentors as part of my professional life, but I have also mentored many individuals, helping them to see new ways to achieve their goals, or giving them a new perspective to see a situation as an opportunity instead of an obstacle.

Mentoring is also a part of how you retain employees while helping them to develop their careers. If your career has put you in a position of leadership, mentoring allows you to develop the talent in your department, which makes you look good, makes your boss look good, and benefits your company. It is truly a win-win for everyone.

Don't limit mentoring to just those who are younger. Use mentoring as a means to make connections with those in your department, company, or industry. You are thus building alliances, increasing your network, while providing potential opportunities to others. The benefits of being a mentor include helping others to measure the success of their efforts. Now let's talk about how you measure your success.

Evaluate Your Success

When it comes to creating change in your career, you need to be able to set markers that help you measure whether you are successfully meeting your goals and progressing in terms of your opportunities, alliances, and overall growth. Scientists create markers to determine how successful an experiment is as part of the process of outlining the experiment itself. You need to be willing to do the same.

Your alliances need to help you to achieve results. You may outline a few markers to help you determine if they are working as you anticipated or if you are not achieving the results that you desired.

I think of sales reports as a great example of what I am talking about. When a sales report is run, you learn how much was sold, and compare it from month to month, quarter to quarter, and year to year. If goals are not being met, they can pinpoint where the problem is.

You need to be just that focused on evaluating your success. Be honest with yourself— brutally so. If you aren't, then you cannot make real change happen. I don't want you to skip the evaluation, because that is giving you a pass to be lazy and not achieve the career that you want. Growth can't happen without assessing what went right and what went wrong.

Wrap Up for Chapter 8 (Constructing a Transformational You)

- Building networks involves creating alliances, both short-term and long-term.
- Have goals in building your network.
- Don't be afraid to let it grow organically, instead of trying to make connections for the sake of connections.
- Your online presence reflects who you are, so be cautious about what you post and how you speak in online communications.
- Finding coaches and mentors can help you in the evaluation process, but you can pay it forward by being a mentor yourself.
- Evaluate your success and be willing to make changes as needed.

Now that you understand the importance of alliances, in *Making Money Means Making More Than Just Money*, I want to focus on how you can turn your avatar on and off, how your avatar impacts your conduct, and what your professional growth can mean for others.

Chapter 9

Making Money Means
Making More Than Just Money

**"Without continual growth and progress,
such words as improvement, achievement,
and success have no meaning."
– Benjamin Franklin**

What you will learn:

- How the money you make can impact others
- Creating a legacy through the actions of your avatar
- Reaching out to others to give them direction

No matter what you do for a career, your professional life is going to be providing the income for you to achieve all your dreams and to fulfill your purpose. Therefore, making money is about more than just making money. It is about funding your lifestyle and your ability to impact others. You can create a legacy, one that allows you to pass on more than financial or professional wisdom: your knowledge, experiences, and values gained from a lifetime journey.

I want to be clear that you don't have to wait until you retire for you to start using the benefits of your avatar to help others. Plus, when you are giving to others, you are creating a joy within yourself that can't be matched.

Think about how you choose to help others. It might be volunteering your spare time at a not-for-profit organization, such as a soup kitchen, homeless shelter, or a program devoted to helping kids find their own passion and purpose. You might also spend time talking to others and getting support for various causes, including environmental ones, or even potential solutions to address the challenges in your community. Perhaps you are devoted to causes for social justice, such rights for different groups, or access to opportunities that are being denied to various individuals.

Those experiences give you a sense of accomplishment and allow you to build a legacy that benefits others far beyond material possessions or a large bank account. How can your brand avatar help you in the process of creating a legacy?

Your professional career gives you the funds and ability to pursue those passions and causes, because you are able to give financial support and care for your own needs as well. Your career might also give you access to connections that allow you to get more attention for your cause. For example, you might be passionate about an aspect of the environment, perhaps conservation of trees. During the course of your career, you might make connections with others who support that vision. Perhaps you are able to influence the buying decisions of your company, by sourcing recycled office supplies, thus supporting your cause of protecting and conserving trees. In the course of your career, you might also end up meeting an executive who could support a grant that protects old growth trees from being harvested. The point is that you can do a lot to support your cause, simply by the influence you wield and the connections you make. That contributes to your legacy, as you leave an example for those who follow you.

Millennials are often seen as the generation that chooses their jobs based on what the company stands for and their ability to support their personal causes, perhaps as part of the company's own outreach into the community. Gone are the days of working just for a paycheck.

Instead, new employees want to match their values and beliefs with their employers.

If your company offers you opportunities to work in the community or support causes that are close to your heart and connect with your purpose, then why not take advantage of those opportunities?

How can your avatar help you to achieve more, in terms of supporting what you value personally? It starts with using your avatar to expand your reach professionally. Yet you need to recognize that your avatar is not meant to take over your life. You are not going to live and breathe your brand avatar 24/7. Instead, you need to understand those times when it is critical to put it on, and when your genuine self needs to shine through instead.

Turning Your Avatar On and Off

When you are at any company event or on the clock, you need to turn that brand avatar on. Focus on your environment and how you can use elements of your avatar to make yourself stand out to your boss and other executives. Granted, there are going to be times when you focus on making them look better, thus helping your boss to look good by your actions and how you carry yourself. The point is that you are focused on using your avatar to benefit your career.

Too often, it is easy to forget how our actions reflect on those in management. Yet how you reflect on your boss can impact whether you are moving forward or not. Let's face it, your boss and his bosses are in control of your ability to receive the opportunities to move upward. When you reflect poorly on them, they are not likely to consider you for advancement, and you could end up being the stumbling block to your own career.

Now let's take that concept and focus on your level of influence in a company or with others in your department. When you don't reflect well on them, then it can be difficult to influence them into supporting your vision or cause. You will find that when you do your best to reflect well on those higher up, and your department as a whole, it will increase your influence and your ability to get things done in other areas.

Clearly, your avatar can be a positive impact on your ability to do what needs to be done, either in a role of support or one where you are gaining influence among those who can have a greater impact on your cause. Still, there are going to be periods of time where your avatar needs to be shut down, and your genuine self needs to come to the fore. I am talking about those times in your life where you are creating meaningful connections. Your brand avatar is something that you take on and off, much like your favorite sweatshirt or your favorite pair of tennis shoes. It is a part of you, but not who you truly are.

Your life purpose, the thing that brings you profound joy and gets you excited to start the day, is truly the core of who you are. Use your brand avatar to compliment that purpose, allowing you to follow through and benefit others in the process.

The reason that I want to address this topic is that you can easily fall into the trap of keeping your avatar on all the time, looking at every situation through the eyes of your brand avatar. The point of your avatar is to help you grow your career, but it shouldn't be at the expense of who you are as a person. After all, it is merely a means to an end, not the end itself.

Bringing my avatar to events where I am now an extension of my department, company, or bosses is beneficial in terms of achieving the perception I want others to have of me. It could be a social situation, an industry event, or even the office party for the boss' birthday. Each situation might call for something different from my brand avatar, but I am always first and foremost focused on the goals I have set for myself, and then use my brand avatar to support those goals and objectives.

You need to remember this as well. Think about how you dress. If you were going to a party with your friends, then you might pull out a comfortable outfit, one that reflects your style and preferences. However, if you are going to an event that is geared around your company, and involves co-workers or clients, you might be more inclined to dress more formally, to shape their perception of you. Dress how you want to be addressed, something that is important always to remember.

It is not about trying to change who you are, but about how you present yourself and thus impact how others view you. Perceptions drive individuals to act in a certain way. I can't even express how many times perceptions have impacted the ability of individuals to move up in their companies and departments. Too often, you are in the driver's seat about how you present yourself to others. Therefore, use your avatar to influence how others perceive you, but don't assume that your avatar can replace your abilities, experiences, and skills.

I want you to remember that you have the power over your avatar, not the other way around. Turning it off can mean many things, but ultimately, turning off your avatar can give you the ability to take a break from your career and focus on yourself and what you can do for others, without expecting anything in return.

Taking Time for You

When you turn your avatar off, I want you to remember that it is merely one part of you, not everything that you are or that you can bring to the table. Too often, you can get lost in your avatar, often at the expense of what brings you joy and contentment. Your career is not your life, but if you do not recognize the importance of turning off your avatar from time to time, you can lose sight of that.

In the movie, *Avatar*, the main character uses an avatar to escape the limitations of his physical body, allowing him to interact with those that are part of another culture and environment. Over time, his interactions changed his thinking about how he wanted to interact with others, including his bosses.

I point this out, because your interactions with others while using your brand avatar, do not occur in a vacuum. You are going to find yourself exposed to new ideas, new ways of doing things, and new influences. How you choose to incorporate them is up to you, but taking time for yourself allows you to process that information and influences, giving you the opportunity to keep what is beneficial and leave the rest behind.

Remember what you are capable of accomplishing with your brand avatar can be beneficial to others. Can you take the time to mentor someone who might be struggling in an area that you have mastered through your trial and error? Perhaps you can coach someone to help them improve in an area of weakness. The point is that you are looking for opportunities to help others, provide support, and thus move the world closer to one that you want to leave behind for others.

It can be so easy to become focused on your goals and objectives for your career and how it benefits you, that you lose sight of how you are impacting others with your avatar. I found it telling that throughout the movie, *Avatar*, there were individuals who had little regard for how their actions were impacting others because they focused only on their goal. That disregard can end up backfiring on you, and negatively impacting all the progress that you may have made with your avatar, but also all the progress you may have made helping others.

Taking time to turn off your avatar can also allow you to recalibrate, based on feedback that you receive from others, and which you observe yourself. As you receive confirmation from others that your efforts to shape their perceptions are working (or not!), then you can make adjustments to support and enhance the response, or to try again to alter it.

The point of this time is to focus on yourself so that you can be better at helping others. Additionally, as you get personal with your avatar, you can pass on a mindset of helping others and create a ripple across a bigger pond than you realize.

Get Personal with Your Avatar

Your avatar should not be a robot, one that you use to interact with others. It is an extension of who you are and your own goals and objectives. You do not want to become mechanical in how you use your avatar. People will feel when you are just going through the motions and not truly connected to the outcome.

Therefore, it is important to remember that when you turn your avatar on, you are making a connection with others that goes beyond a superficial one. You do not want to be perceived as fake or disingenuous. When those in power get that perception of you, it can be very difficult to persuade them that you are connected to the goals and objectives of the company, or that you are going to do much to help move them forward.

Appearances are everything! You are not doing this just to make money, but you are doing it to make a difference in your life and the lives of others. You are trying to leave a legacy behind, but if you aren't careful with how you use your avatar, it could be a case of self-sabotage. If you are not aware of your conduct and how you appear, then you will find that your avatar is not as effective as you may have planned.

Getting personal with your avatar is recognizing the impact that your avatar can have on others, and how you can influence them to do things differently, to make changes in their own lives, and then give them the desire to assist others in the same way that you helped them. It's that ripple effect. You want to use your avatar to start a chain reaction, one that can help you grow and inspire others to do the same.

Your definition of success is important here. I want you to recognize that success can mean different things to different people. However, most often, those who feel the most successful have that feeling because they did what they could to connect to others. They built relationships, gave back, and passed on something to the next generation. It is a measure of success if you leave a legacy that gives others the tools to grow in an area that you may have only been able to plant but not harvest.

Think of all the ways that you are building on the efforts of those who came before you. After you are gone, are you leaving a platform that someone else can use to go a little bit higher, or travel a little bit further? I want you to give this some thought because the tools I am giving you can have a far greater impact than just on your career. It can give you the ability to impact many individuals, some you might not even be aware of.

So how can you be sure that your avatar is successful in doing what you need to do to create the opportunities that you hope will lead to achieving your definition of success? It starts by being aware of your conduct, both with your avatar on and your avatar off.

Watch Your Conduct 24/7

The reason that I bring up your conduct is because that is what individuals base their perceptions on. It is simply the reality of any professional environment. Therefore, when you put on your avatar, you need to recognize that your conduct will be judged, just as if you didn't have your avatar on at all.

Let's go to that office party again. Did you take advantage of that open bar, imbibing rather liberally? How did you behave afterward? Is it a YouTube type of moment, one that gives you notoriety that you wish you didn't have? Nothing ever gets erased from the internet, but you might as well say the same thing about your reputation in your company. It is hard to build one that will help you to reach your goals, and damnably easy to ruin that hard work with just one night of wild abandonment.

Watching your conduct, even when others are not making good choices, can help you to stand out positively. However, you want to be sure that you aren't creating a reputation of always being stuck up or avoiding those who have a good time. The principle here, one that you need to keep as a guiding light, is that moderation is key.

How you use your avatar needs to be in moderation in terms of how it impacts your goals and objectives. Your conduct also needs to have moderation to it. You want to remember that how you act today will have an impact on how you are treated in the days to follow.

I often speak of informal company gatherings, but you can also apply this principle to formal company gatherings as well. Think of that company meeting where your boss was pitching an idea, one with a potentially high degree of risk. Did you provide support, giving him the information necessary to present the idea effectively to those who are decision makers? Or did you withhold that support by not being as prepared as you should have been?

On the other hand, are you perhaps reflecting badly because you are talking over your boss, not allowing him to lead the meeting as he sees fit? You might find that you leave a bad taste in the mouth of those who are in positions of leadership if you are seen to defy them or appear to be trying to make them look bad. Choose your battles wisely. If you have legitimate concerns or issues, then choose an appropriate time to address them. No, a meeting with all the executives would probably not be the right time for that kind of discussion. Remember, the point is to make your boss look good, not look stupid or ill-prepared.

As you can see, the importance of your avatar is wrapped up in how you use it and when you take it off. Your conduct is critical because of the impact that it can have; so, do not be quick to dismiss the power you have in guarding your conduct throughout the various interactions that you have with others, both personally and professionally.

In the end, you are creating an avatar for a purpose, one that goes beyond how much money you make. Your avatar is helping you to achieve your professional dreams and goals so that you can achieve your personal ones.

Those personal goals are wrapped up in what you can give to others and the legacy you can build. I want you to remember that you will find a greater joy in passing on wisdom and knowledge than just passing on material wealth. Your legacy is in the platform you leave behind, and in the example, you give others to follow.

Wrap Up for Chapter 9 (Making Money Means Making More Than Just Money)

• Turning your avatar on and off allows you to make adjustments and to keep your avatar effective.
• Take time to care for yourself and your needs, to be able to wield your brand avatar effectively.
• Watch your conduct, as it can have a greater impact than you realize on the effectiveness of your avatar.
• Remember that your avatar helps you in the professional arena, thus giving you the resources to achieve your life's purpose and passions.

Throughout these chapters, I have focused on a variety of aspects related to building a brand avatar and creating a network to support that avatar. Now, I want you to remember that this is an exercise in continuous improvement. In the final chapter, *Rinse and Repeat, Rinse and Repeat*, I will focus on how you can put continuous improvement on your side, and the benefits of using your brand avatar to reach the next level of your career, which will help you to keep your brand avatar relevant.

Chapter 10

Rinse and Repeat, Rinse and Repeat

"The journey is never ending. There's always gonna be growth, improvement, adversity; you just gotta take it all in and do what's right, continue to grow, continue to live in the moment."
– Antonio Brown

What you will learn:

- Why your brand avatar is important to creating opportunities
- Keep adjusting your avatar to reflect your changing goals and objectives
- Focus on mastering your environment to maximize the impact of your avatar
- Remember that perceptions are key and should play a part in your alliances and online interactions

Throughout these chapters, I have focused on creating a brand avatar, and the best ways to put that avatar to work in creating the career you want, to support the life you want to live. It is not a simple process that involves just one action or another and the work is done. Instead, you are going to find that you need to think, plan, act, analyze, and then start the process all over again.

As you progress through your life, your goals and the focus of your life are going to change, because you are going to be changed by your experiences. There is no such thing as truly living a stagnant life, unless you choose to do so.

Therefore, I want to ask you a question. Where do you want to go? Is the current trajectory of your career going to take you where you want to go, or is it going to hinder your progress? Too many times, we have aspirations and dreams, and visions of the type of life we want to live. In the end, we sell ourselves short, just because we end up choosing the path of least resistance, or do not act in harmony with those dreams, goals, and visions.

I want you to use your brand avatar to avoid having disconnect between where you want to go and where you are headed, based on your current actions. There is a reason why some individuals dream, but others live their dreams. They find a way to make sure that their dreams turn into their reality, based on their actions.

My focus throughout this book was to help you line up your actions with your goals and dreams. Your avatar is simply one weapon that you have in your professional arsenal. Still, it is important to remember that your professional life is just one aspect of your life as a whole. The progress you make professionally is meant to benefit you personally, giving you the resources to pursue your passions and the things that make you whole.

At the Start of Our Journey

Right from the beginning, I wanted to get you focused on the benefits of a brand avatar and what it means. Branding is an art, one that companies regularly use to achieve their goals and communicate their message effectively. I want you to recognize that you can create your brand, one that is meant to benefit you professionally and can give you the ability to stand out from those around you.

Before you can create a brand, however, you need to understand what you are branding and why. When you take the time to get to know yourself, then you begin to understand the message that you want to communicate, and how you want to present yourself. Along with understanding what you want your brand to be, it is important to remember that the world has a perception of who you are and what you bring to the table. When you understand how you are perceived, then you can take the actions necessary to change it.

At the same time, the point of the brand avatar is to allow you to be consistent in your messaging. You are not going just to make it up as you go along on professional journey. You need to train yourself to present a consistent message and set of actions through your avatar. It is about creating a voice and vision, which can be used to assist you in meeting your goals and objectives.

A portion of the process is about refining your message, recognizing that you are the one who can define your path, not others. You need to know what you want to accomplish and where you want to go, not what you believe is expected of you or what you think others want you to accomplish.

Creating a plan for success starts with defining your ultimate goals. Your plan will be the best way to achieve those ultimate goals and will give you objectives that are going to help you determine if you are making progress toward that goal, or are simply dead in the water.

Part of any plan is the level of encouragement you give yourself to keep going during the difficult times. When I think of vision boarding and affirmations, I see them as part of the process of keeping myself focused on the goal, even if I am dealing with difficult circumstances at the moment.

For everyone that wants to see you succeed, there are just as many individuals who want to see you fall flat on your face. You know them by their negative comments, negative way of thinking, and the fact that it seems like no matter how joyful the news, they always find a way to put a damper on it. I want you to remember that those individuals are going to suck energy out of your avatar. In any video game, avatars have only so much energy. You need to manage it effectively to win the game.

It is the same when you are talking about your career. You need to manage your avatar's energy by avoiding prolonged exposure to negativity. Constructive criticism is one thing, but negative thinking is another; one can build you up, while the other tears you down.

Throughout a video game, there are always places where you can collect additional energy, giving your avatar new strength or the ability to keep going. Look for positive people who are imparting information and guidance that can help you move forward. In your personal and professional lives, you will find that positive people are going to give off an energy that can help you to get excited, motivated, and energized.

The point is not to avoid certain people entirely, as you are likely working with a few of those negative individuals right now, but the point is to do what is necessary to avoid allowing that negativity to sap your energy and your ability to get things done.

Creating an Ideal Universe Starts with You

As I started this journey with you, I focused on you, and how to build your brand avatar. Along the way, I shared ways that you could use your brand avatar effectively, and how you needed to stay true to who you are. Then I moved on to understanding your environment.

During this part of our journey together, I wanted you to take away the fact that you can operate in any environment, using your brand avatar. It is simply a question of taking your knowledge of the environment and putting it to work for you. Don't work against the environment you are presented within your office or department.

You might be able to create change in your department, and you could have the best idea, but if you don't work within the environment and culture of the department, it is going to be hard for you to get others to accept your idea or way of thinking. The point is to get them on your side and expand your influence to create real change. Your avatar is a reflection of who you are, but also a reflection of where you want to go. Use it to build the relationships that will help you to get there.

I love working with individuals and helping them to master their environment. Too often, they have some or all the pieces needed to be truly successful, but they haven't put them together. Working with a mentor, someone who has already been where you are, can be a way to help you tap into the skills that you have, and give you the ability to direct them effectively.

You may also choose to work with a coach, just to develop a specific skill or to strengthen a weakness that you have found in your abilities. When you take the time to work with these types of individuals, you are giving yourself the leg up to help you stand out from the rest. Not everyone takes advantage of a coach or a mentor. They think their abilities are enough to help them take the next step in their careers. I am here to tell you that if you are not open to the idea and willing to work with a mentor or a coach, then you are handicapping your success.

Give your avatar every advantage to maximize your success. One of the key ways that I focused on maximizing your success potential is learning o deal with frustrations in your department. We all are faced with them, but the question is how to deal with them in such a way that it can benefit you in the long run. I want you to remember that your frustrations can be the fuel you need to create real change or to spur your career forward.

You might not be able to change the person or circumstances frustrating you directly, but by not succumbing to your frustration, you can act in such a way that you might be able to make a difference in how individuals interact with you. Recognize that frustration is often related to your perception of the individual or circumstances. If you can alter your perceptions, then you can also alter your frustrations.

Finally, your avatar is the way you interact with your environment, so you need to be flexible. Part of my discussion in Chapter 7 was a focus on being a lemming, a rebel, or a leader, depending on the circumstances. When you master your environment, then you can use the one that is the right fit for the situation. Never assume that you are locked into being one or the other forever. Remember, the point is to be flexible and able to roll with the changing environment. Too often, those who want to be successful find themselves hindered by their inability to roll with the punches and accept change.

Now I want you to think about a situation at work that is frustrating you. Here are a few key points to keep in mind that can assist you in addressing it effectively.

- Is part of your frustration related to your inability to be flexible to the changing environment?
- Do you know your department norms, or is your lack of knowledge of the environment negatively impacting your ability to be successful, thus increasing your frustration?
- Are you productive in your environment in a way that supports your vision, or are you simply moving around without making progress?

To stand out in the crowd, you need to understand the environment, and then do what is necessary to highlight your skills and how they can make your boss look good. I realize that you might think it is counterproductive to make your boss look good, without necessarily getting the credit, but the truth is that your boss can be a way to open doors of opportunity. When you work with them, instead of against them, they are more likely to consider you for promotions or other projects that give you a chance to shine.

Never underestimate the power of perception. It is critical to your success. As you think about how you are perceived, remember that mentors can give you an objective point of view. Using this point of view, you can make adjustments to shore up your avatar in areas that might be negatively impacting your advancement.

Take Your Brand Avatar to the Next Level

Once you create your avatar, it is time to put it to use in the environment that you have taken the time to learn. I called it the *construction of a transformational you*. At this point, your avatar is the key to building the right perceptions of who you are and where you want to go.

Part of putting on your avatar involves building alliances, and then doing what is necessary to support them. In Chapter 8, I also drew your attention to the impact of various alliances on your progress or lack of it. By focusing on your alliances, you can find the ones that you need to limit your interactions with and those alliances that you need to cultivate.

Throughout this chapter, I also pointed out how you can be impacted by what you choose to put online, in a variety of ways, not just social media. Just pick up the paper, or click on your favorite news source, to find stories of how individuals tripped up their careers, just by what they posted online or by the emails they sent. I encourage you to avoid posting or sharing information about your political views, your religious affiliations, or jokes that are greater than PG rated. They can come back to bite you, either in a loss of promotions or even your job disappearing altogether. By keeping these rules in mind, you can keep yourself from making an error in judgment or putting yourself in a position that will stop you from moving forward.

With that being said, I want to draw your attention back to the idea of coaching or mentoring. Each of them gives you specific benefits, so don't be afraid to take advantage of both of them. Once you do, you will find that you quickly create opportunities that you might have missed otherwise. Plus, you can maximize your strengths and shore up weaknesses that may be negatively impacting your progress.

Finally, the idea is that your success is not just about your career but about giving you the resources to help others. Do not assume that your success is limited only to achieving your goals and dreams, but it can give you the tools to allow others to find their success. Your legacy is not what you achieve to make your own life better but what you can pass onto others.

Think about ways that you could mentor or perhaps coach someone else. Other ways to pass on your knowledge and abilities could come through volunteering or working with a charity or cause that appeals to your passions. I want you to get excited about how you can turn your success into a stepping stone for someone else.

This is my favorite part of my avatar because I can have fun teaching others and give them the benefit of my experience. When you are successful, you leave a path for someone else to follow. I taught you how to build an avatar and how to use it successfully to build your career, but those skills and knowledge are not limited. You can take them and help others to make progress as well. Do not see your avatar as something you need to use for only a short period. Keep using it throughout your career. Allow it to be a part of your strategy to connect with others and achieve your goals and objectives.

Let your avatar become a tool that you use over and over again, recalibrating it as necessary. This is the rinse and repeat aspect of our discussion. If you do not continually practice or make efforts to improve your avatar, then you will find only limited success in using one. My task is to help you to understand how you can improve your avatar, and how to make rinse and repeat part of your path to success.

Your life purpose is wrapped up in what you focus on and how you choose to spend your time. When your career is part of that purpose, your avatar can be part of the path that you follow to achieve that purpose. Whoever you are, your purpose is likely not limited to your own dreams, or definition of success, but involves how you can benefit others. Time and again, I see how a purpose greater than ourselves can positively impact our lives, giving us a level of joy that those without a connection to their life purpose simply don't have.

It is about knowing what you really want, setting an overarching goal, and then defining all the mini-goals that can help you see if you are heading in the right direction, as well as helping you to achieve your overarching goal. How do you eat an elephant? One bite at a time. Don't allow yourself to be overwhelmed, but instead, you can see those smaller goals as the bites that make it easier to achieve your ultimate goal.

As part of my vision for your avatar, I want to offer you some additional tools and opportunities at **www.poolofwealth.com**. Here, I provide you with personal branding tools, free access to money making opportunities, and self-help programs to give you a leg up as you build your avatar and put it to work for you.

This is an exciting time for you! I hope you are inspired to see beyond where you are in your career, to see where you could be, and how you can achieve whatever you envision. There are no limits, and with these tools, tips, and skills, you are in a position to create the reality that you want, not the one that is defined by someone else.

I want to work with you, giving you the benefit of my experiences in building my brand avatar, and allow you to use your avatar to achieve your purpose. There is always more that you can do with your avatar; and to that end, I am available to work with you, via my website, **www.poolofwealth.com** or Google Duane Browne to add me to your favorite social media outlet.

I look forward to working with you and helping you to take your avatar to the next level, giving you the ability to reach your goals and connect with your purpose! Recognize that you have unique abilities and talents. With the right branding approach, you can let others see you in a whole new light, and you can show others *Unlock Your Professional Potential & Dramatically Increase Your Income!*

Duane Browne

Wrap Up for Chapter 10 (Rinse and Repeat, Rinse and Repeat)

- Your brand avatar is an important part of creating opportunities in personal and professional areas of your life.
- Your brand avatar should always be adjusting to reflect the continuing changing of your goals and objectives.
- Mastering your environment is key to maximizing the impact of your avatar, particularly in your professional life.
- Perceptions are key and should play a part in the types of alliances and online interactions that you participate in.

Chapter 11

(Pool Of Wealth Secret Chapter)
The Urban Planner

**"The critical ingredient is getting off your butt
and doing something. It's as simple as that.
A lot of people have ideas, but there are few who decide
to do something about them now. Not tomorrow.
Not next week. But today.
The true entrepreneur is a doer, not a dreamer."
– Nolan Bushnell**

What you will learn:

- Why the fastest way to success in your career is through intra and entrepreneurship
- Tools I used (and you can too) to create a new career environment while I was an employee
- What is your BHAG & how can intra and entrepreneurship help you reach your professional goals?
- What is your why for living?

For those who have heard of Kevin Hart, he is one of the most talented comedians of my generation. Now I do not know him personally, so I can not comment on anything he does other than what I have seen onstage or in social media. I do, however, remember him doing an interview where he spoke about how his mother provided the help that he needed to literally transform his life. As the story goes, Kevin Hart was questioning his ability to make a living as a comedian and was unable to pay his bills. Looking to his mother for support, he did not get what he expected. All she said was, "Kevin, did you read your Bible?" Feeling like she was no help, he went about his business trying to make it as a comedian and trying to make ends meet. Things got worse, so he again asked his mother for help and she replied, "Kevin, did you read your Bible?"

As any person looking for help, when you get an answer that you feel does not address your situation, you tend to get a little angry and frustrated. So did Kevin. He was frustrated and a bit annoyed that all his mother could say was to read his Bible when he needed real world help. Then came his breaking point. After months of struggling and not being able to support himself, he decided to listen to his mother and read his Bible, in the hope some sort of inspiration would come his way. As he opened the Bible, there waiting for him was 6 months worth of rent. Kevin's mother put money in his Bible and was trying to teach him a lesson, that the best blessings tend to be lessons in disguise. Why do I share this story with you? I do it to show that when you follow instructions, are coachable, and trust in your network for support, you can achieve magical results. This chapter is for anyone who took the time to read the book and is ready to take their life to the next level.

This book is about creating an Avatar for your personal brand, so you can unlock your professional potential and drastically increase your income. Now what happens, if after you apply all the suggestions in the book, increase your income and corporate exposure, but you are still feeling unfulfilled? If that is the case, then it is fitting that this chapter is Chapter 11. In business, a Chapter 11 is the reorganization of a debtor's business affairs, debts, and assets. That is exactly what you must do. Reorganize your business affairs and determine your *why* in life. If you had the power, what would your big hairy audacious goals (BHAG) be? This process can only be accomplished through intra and entrepreneurship.

Intra and Entrepreneurship

Let's just cut to the chase. There is a direct relationship between massive success in business and being the owner of that business. If the company is publicly traded, you can still have massive success, but you are at the mercy of shareholders and board members. The key is to find the balance to create the life that you want. Before I get into it, let's briefly define intrapreneurship and entrepreneurship.

Intrapreneurship: Is the act of behaving like an entrepreneur while working within a large organization. Intrapreneurship is known as the practice of a corporate management style that integrates risk-taking and innovation approaches, as well as the reward and motivational techniques, that are more traditionally thought of as being the province of entrepreneurship. - **Wikipedia**

I like this option of career development as it acts almost like "on the job" training to pivot to your own business with the comfort that the organization has resources to help you manage risks. It allows you to practise your leadership skills and freedom to transform innovative ideas into actionable tactics, which is essentially your creative faculties at play. Typically, you are compensated very well in these types of roles. Let's be clear that you still work for someone else (meaning you are not immune to being laid off). What I will say is you can do a lot for your BHAG development. All ultimate goals start with many mini goals that build the foundation blocks for achieving your ultimate goal. If you are in an organization, seek out the thought leaders and executives to learn from their expertise. Volunteer for them, gain their trust and follow their counsel. In-company mentors will be vital if you are to emerge as a solid intrapreneur in the company. When you have innovation on the mind, try to remove all ego from the equation. It is not always about what you did, it is more about how you contributed to the cause. At times you may get zero credit for your efforts. Let it serve to help motivate and move you from intra to entre in the development of your professional greatness.

Entrepreneurship: is the process of designing, launching, and running a new business, which is often initially a small business. The people who create these businesses are called entrepreneurs. - **Wikipedia**

This is where the magic really happens. This is the wind beneath my wings moment (credit to Bette Midler). As an entrepreneur you reap all the benefits of your creative vision as you take action to move your vision into something that solves a problem or desire for your targeted audience. The more value you provide, the more the level of success potential you can attain. If you have ever second guessed your ability to be an entrepreneur, think of it this way. Any job you have ever worked was given to you because they thought you could do it. Now they did not hire you because they liked you (even though it could be a contributing factor), they hired you because they required help and the premise was that you could assist them in that regard. The ultimate way to unlock your professional potential and drastically increase your income is through entrepreneurship. My book *"3 Steps to Riches"* (available at **www.poolofwealth.com**), gives you some tools to get you from point A – Z in an easy to understand manner. The 3 steps are:

1. Find something you are passionate about.
2. Set action-oriented goals to get started on your business related to that passion.
3. Create a support system to help and mentor you on your path to success.

3 Steps to Riches is a must have and must read for anyone who feels that entrepreneurship is too daunting a task to take on. This book is for ANYONE in this world with out of this world dreams and desires. It also has some bonuses you will enjoy that provide an honest look into my past. I hope you never have to learn some of the hard life lessons I had to learn. Always remember, you were created to prosper, and being an entrepreneur will get you there.

Tools for Business Success

There are many tools (paid and free) on the market that will help you increase your speed to success. In my efforts to make this book ever fresh (meaning good today, tomorrow and 30 years from now), I want to be as generic as possible. With that being said, there are some free tools I want to discuss to help get you started. These tools will help you be more productive, more informed, and more connected.

My Favourite Productivity Tools

When it comes to being productive, I think one of the most important tools you can have is an up to date calendar. Not only should it be up to date, it should have tasks broken down by importance, urgency and strategic alignment. I personally create daily meetings with myself in the morning to pray, do my morning meditation and do controlled breathing. These meeting makers come complete with reminders and ring tones to ensure I stick with the planned time to prep my day. Inputting everything you would like to do also produces structure to your days and weeks. It allows you to see right before your eyes if you are not doing enough in your day or doing way too much (and if you should delegate some of that).

Another way to remain productive is to keep a high level of energy throughout your day. When your mind, body and soul are tired or lacking energy it is impossible to give 100% in what you are doing. So how do you manufacture energy when you are already operating at less than 100%? The answer is:

- Get meaningful sleep
- Have a morning routine
- Create lists

Getting enough sleep is less about the number of hours you get in as it is about the quality of your sleep. I am by no means a sleep expert;

however, what I will tell you is it does not matter what someone tells you about sleep and success, your body needs it to recharge and regenerate itself. Some people operate off 8 hours, some 7, 6 or even 5 hours. In order to get that good rem sleep, you need to prep yourself for sleep. Avoid looking at any electronic devices 30 minutes before bed. This will eliminate the tendency of your brain to still be actively computing the information coming at it while you are sleeping. Try to put yourself in reflective mode where you are thinking about all the positive wins in the day. If you had a tough day, try being grateful for being alive. Be grateful for that breath you just took, be grateful that tomorrow is another day to strive for excellence.

I would also suggest you investigate your sleep patterns. Find a sleep doctor who can help you determine if you need any sleep assistance (such as pillow for stomach sleepers or nose strips to increase oxygen to the brain). I had a good friend who always woke up tired even when he had 8 hours sleep. After working with a sleep doctor, he discovered that in a given night, he woke up well over 50 times. How does one get a good night's sleep when they are waking up 50 times a night? After going through a sleep program, he now wakes up with so much energy it is like he is a new person. He is more productive in the morning and he starts his day with more conviction and determination than ever.

The first thing you should do every morning is be thankful you woke up. Many people go to bed at night and never wake up (so be thankful you live to see another day). The second thing you should do right away is drink a glass of water. Your body is mainly water and you must first deal with hydration and internal nourishment of the body. Do these things before you even start your official morning routine. I call this the pre-game set up for success. Now that you have done this, you can start with your morning routine.

The magical thing about having a morning routine is after a while you will be able to do it on auto-pilot without even thinking about all the positive impacts it is having on your success. Your morning routine is not just a process, it is a conscious decision to do activities that benefit your mind, body and soul. When you wake up you should put yourself in gratitude mode. There are many ways to do that but for me the easiest way is to meditate and reflect in the shower. Think of the water as blessings raining down on you. Give thanks for everything you have and will have in your future. Get excited for the day. If you have to create something to get excited about, do so. As I right this book, I am excited for the treat I am giving myself come lunchtime (as simple as that is, positive energy is contagious, and it expands the more you use it). Below is a cheat sheet of my routine that has served me create amazing days, every day.

Duane Browne's night routine:

1. Write down top 3 tasks to accomplish for the next day.
    This will help start your day tomorrow

2. Drink a glass of water.
    Help lubricate your internal organs as you start your deep fast (sleep)

3. Stop looking at any electronics at least 30 minutes before I close my eyes.
    Settle your mind and prepare for mind and body to self heal itself

4. Spend 10 minutes meditating.
    Take a conscious step to calm the mind, set intentions and centre yourself

5. Spend 5 minutes in prayer or spiritual reflection.
    This might not be important to all but it is important to me personally

6. Ensure the room is in complete darkness.
    Helps with Rem sleep

7. While I lay in bed, daydream about my goals and desires (mental vision boarding).
    My sweet spot is 8-9 hours of sleep. Yours might be more or less. If you need to go to bed earlier then do so

With that last point, I know at times I will have moments of little to no sleep as I go after my goals and dreams but if I want to wake up at 6am (early bird gets the worm), then 9:30am – 10:00am is a good time to get to bed.

Duane Browne's morning routine:

1. Give thanks for waking up, be grateful for family friends, health, wealth and success.
    Always give thanks for your life. Every day is a gift from the universe

2. Spend no more than 15 minutes in bed after alarm goes off.
    You set that time for a reason, so honour that time and get up and get going

3. Make up my bed.
    First quick win of the day

4. Drink a glass of water and take my vitamins.
    Water is vital to your body getting off to a fresh start. Vitamins help supercharge it

5. Do push ups and jumping jacks while listening to motivational audio books.
    It is important to exercise your body as well as your mind

6. Take a shower while I "thinkitate," pray and verbally declare my goals.
    There is something magical on thinking and goal setting in the shower

7. Review my top 3 to do list (which I set the night before).
    Level setting on what is important for the day will set the tone for the rest of the day

8. Aim to get as close to a 16 hour fast before I eat breakfast.
    There is a regenerative power in allowing your body to heal itself without interruption

9. Before I start my day, spend 15 minutes meditating & in prayer.
    This might not be important to all but it is important to me personally

10. Spend 10-15 minutes reading self development books/literature.
    Growing and learning is essential for all growth

As part of my morning routine and throughout the day, my secret to success is in my list, highlighting the most important thing I MUST do for the day, then the next important thing I MUST do. All successful people know the importance of jotting down tasks to accomplish daily, weekly, and monthly goals. The great thing about creating a list is you can integrate it into your calendar. I would also suggest getting yourself an accountability partner to follow up on your list and progress. No one is an island and without confiding in someone to help keep you motivated and on track, you will never reach your place of greatness.

I think the best productivity tool which also happens to have the best ROI is mapping out how you spend your travel time to and from work. This is your time to educate yourself, stimulate yourself and add time back in your day. If you drive to work, you should have audio programs to help with your self-improvement. Same thing if you walk to work, have audio programs loaded on your smartphone. If you take the bus or train to work, you have the added bonus of being able to write, type and craft your business plans, operations and goals.

Your BHAG

Earlier I mentioned that BHAG is your big, hairy, audacious goal. I learned this term from one of my mentors, Pete Vargas. He urged me to let my creative mind be free to think about a goal that I would set with no barriers, no limits, and one that impacted others in a positive way. My BHAG is:

1. Donate at minimum, $1 million dollars of my own money every year to those in need
2. To mentor (directly or indirectly) 1 million people
3. To travel the world helping others attain financial freedom or at least help to increase their financial literacy

What is your BHAG? Make it something wild, extravagant and something that adds value to others. Focus on them. If you had all the money in the world, who would you help and how would you improve the world beyond what you could do for your family and friends?

When you start thinking along these lines, then you will find that your thoughts will drive your dreams and actions. This can mean amazing things will be possible in your reality, because you will draw them to yourself like a loadstone or magnet.

What is Your *Why*?

Defining your *why* brings clarity on what drives you to get moving every morning. What motivates and inspires you? It is critical to connect with this part of yourself, because it drives all your aspects of creation and inspires change in all areas of your life.

Embrace the amazing purpose, the why, that motivates you through the process of creating a life that inspires others and leaves a legacy of hope for those who come after you, in both your personal and professional life.

My focus is to give you the tools to take the next steps in creating a personal brand that will help you reach your professional aspirations, but these tools can also be put to use in your personal relationships as well. Reorganize every part of your life to build on initial successes and see where they take you. The journey is beginning, and the road can take you to places you can't even imagine right now. Be open and enjoy this incredible adventure!

Wrap Up for Chapter 11 (The Urban Planner)

- What is your *why* for living?
- Identify your Big Hairy Audacious Goal (BHAG).
- Use your business tools for success to drive your success in your personal life.
- Create massive success with a combination of intrapreneurship and entrepreneurship.

Finally, as I close this book, I want you to recognize the limitless possibilities that are available in your life. You are a unique and amazing individual that can offer so much to the world. Each of us contributes in ways that advance humanity. It is up to you to decide what your contribution will be, and the legacy that you will leave. Now is the time to act on your vision and use your foundation to build a life that capitalizes on your potential. Go out and conquer!

"Your work is going to fill a large part of your life, and the only way to be truly satisfied is to do what you believe is great work.
And the only way to do great work is to love what you do."
– Steve Jobs

Authors' Bios

Raymond Aaron is a New York Times Top 10 bestselling author, investor, business owner and internationally renowned thought leader and success coach. His techniques have generated over $160,000,000.00 from the sale of products and services and over 1100 investment properties valued over $500,000,000.00.

Raymond has committed his life to teaching people how to dramatically change their lives for the better. Raymond transforms lives by helping people tap into their own potential.

Today, Raymond is helping people achieve greater wealth, branding, recognition, confidence, respect and authority. Raymond teaches his clients how to become respected authorities and experts in their fields.

Raymond has shared his vision and wisdom on radio and television programs. He is the author of 8 bestselling books, including *Branding Small Business For Dummies, Double Your Income Doing What You Love* and the Canadian bestseller, *Chicken Soup for the Canadian Soul*. He is the co-author of New York Times bestseller *Chicken Soup for the Parent's Soul.* He is also an avid adventurer, having completed one of the world's toughest races, Polar Race (a 350 mile foot race to the Magnetic North Pole).

Duane Browne is an author, entrepreneur, guest lecturer on branding and marketing techniques, and a mentor with expertise in corporate and consumer branding. Throughout his career, Duane focused on communication, management, and personal leadership. He continues to provide mentoring opportunities to those who want to improve in various areas to create professional excellence.

His professional experience includes building alliances, strategic and tactical planning, creative idea generation, motivational coaching, and management at various stages of the production and sales processes. Additionally, Duane works with individuals to help them develop professionally, providing a resource for employees looking to progress.

Mr. Browne is also involved in his community, serving on various boards and as a guest speaker for charities and other organizations. His goal is to effectively communicate marketing principles while providing transformational experiences to all stakeholders.

He is also the author of *3 Steps to Riches* as well as a couple of children's books geared to inspire kids.. Mr. Browne also served as a part-time marketing professor at Conestoga College.

If you or your organization requires a dynamic speaker, brand coach, marketing strategist, or mentor, Duane Browne is ready to guide you on the path to increased success in business and life. He can be contacted at **www.poolofwealth.com**.

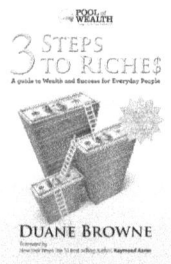

Duane Browne's latest book called
*3 Steps to Riches: A Guide to Wealth
and Success for Everyday People*
is also available.

www.ingramcontent.com/pod-product-compliance
Lightning Source LLC
Chambersburg PA
CBHW050107210326
41519CB00015BA/3854